THE AESTHETICS OF JAMES JOYCE

THE AESTHETICS OF
James Joyce

by

JACQUES AUBERT

·

THE

JOHNS HOPKINS

UNIVERSITY PRESS

Baltimore & London

FOR VONETTE AND LAURENT
with love

Originally published as
Introduction à L'Esthétique de James Joyce
© Librairie Marcel Didier, Paris, 1973

This revised English-language edition © 1992
by The Johns Hopkins University Press

The Johns Hopkins University Press
701 West 40th Street
Baltimore, Maryland 21211-2190
The Johns Hopkins Press Ltd., London

Library of Congress Cataloging-in-Publication Data

Aubert, Jacques.
[Introduction à l'esthétique de James Joyce. English]
The aesthetics of James Joyce / Jacques Aubert.
p. cm.
Translation of: Introduction à l'esthétique de James Joyce.
Includes bibliographical references and index.
ISBN 0-8018-4349-9
1. Joyce, James, 1882–1941—Aesthetics. 2. Aesthetics,
Modern—20th century. I. Title.
PR6019.O9Z5256513 1992
823'.912—dc20 91-45690

74038

CONTENTS

·

CONTENTS

PREFACE

.

JAMES JOYCE produced a body of creative masterpieces which changed the course of literary history and, by the same token, the relationship of both writer and reader to literary texts. Remarkably enough, the general reader most often does not know, and the pedagogue makes haste to forget, that Joyce had been at pains to create a critical concept of the epiphany. Not that this fact did not have the widest circulation, but it has remained isolated and has never been brought to bear on—or become part of—more general critical systems or historical reviews, partly because it has proved practically useless in assessing Joyce's originality and achievement. Another reason may be the uneasy conscience of critics, who feel guilty about looking over Joyce's shoulder: for Joyce's only mention and definition of the epiphany, by now well publicized, occurs in *Stephen Hero,* the early version of *A Portrait of the Artist as a Young Man,* which Joyce energetically refused to publish and which saw the light of day only after his death.

The paradox, then, is that Joyce's only contribution to critical theory lies in a submerged part of his production and that this disappearance is not accidental. His attitude suggests deliberate rejection, the final gesture perhaps in an individual adventure. In other words, what requires attention is the epiphany as manifestation of an absence in a theoretical investigation. The aim of this book, accordingly, is to take seriously the available early material, with a view to discerning, among the tangle of juvenile enthusiasms and tentative constructions, the secret line of research which was specifically Joyce's own.

The task is a difficult one. We suffer from an overabundance of possible sources. For we may safely assume, from internal as well as external evidence, that Joyce had read all that a brilliant young student at the end of the nineteenth century was likely to read of current critical literature, whether romantic (e.g., Coleridge and Shelley) or postromantic (e.g., Ruskin, Pater, and Wilde). No doubt one must be wary of words such as *critical* or *criticism,* which suggest topical—if not contingent—journalistic activity, or a very specific philosophical position that Joyce scarcely mentioned, *a fortiori* held. This does not mean that we must follow him blindfolded when he poses as an Aristotelian or a Thomist, or both. And yet the word *aesthetic,* which he did use, raises the problem of his relation, as a turn-of-the-century author, to Aestheticism and the so-called Aesthetic school. Although the movement had already run its course when he began to write, its impact and part of its legacy certainly outlasted its demise—and that of Oscar Wilde.

In short, I try to steer between the rocks of literary tradition and history and the fascinating maelstrom of philosophical speculation, the aim ultimately being to discover the rationale of what was for Joyce, at the outset of his career, a deeply engrossing line of personal investigation.

ABBREVIATIONS

•

CW   *The Critical Writings of James Joyce*. Edited by Ellsworth Mason and Richard Ellmann. New York: Viking Press, 1959.

Letters   Joyce, James. *Letters of James Joyce*. Edited by Stuart Gilbert (vol. 1, 1957) and Richard Ellmann (vols. 2 and 3, 1966). 3 vols. New York: Viking Press, 1966.

PA   Joyce, James. *A Portrait of the Artist as a Young Man: The Definitive Text, Corrected from the Dublin Holograph*. By Chester G. Anderson and edited by Richard Ellmann. New York: Viking Press, 1964.

SH   Joyce, James. *Stephen Hero*. Edited by John Slocum and Herbert Cahoon. New York: New Directions, 1944; rev. ed., 1963.

U   Joyce, James. *Ulysses*. New York: Random House, 1934; reset and corrected, 1961.

Workshop   *The Workshop of Daedalus: James Joyce and the Raw Materials for "A Portrait of the Artist as a Young Man."* Collected and edited by Robert Scholes and Richard M. Kain. Evanston: Northwestern University Press, 1965.

MBK   Joyce, Stanislaus. *My Brother's Keeper*. Edited, with an Introduction, by Richard Ellmann, and with a Preface by T. S. Eliot. London: Faber & Faber, 1958.

Bosanquet   Bosanquet, Bernard. *A History of Aesthetic*. 1892. Reprint. London: Macmillan, 1904.

Butcher   Butcher, S. H. *Aristotle's Theory of Poetry and Fine Art*. London: Macmillan, 1895, 1897; rev. ed., 1902.

Oeuvres   Joyce, James. *Oeuvres*. Edited by Jacques Aubert. Vol. 1. Paris: Gallimard, Bibliothèque de la Pléiade, 1982.

THE AESTHETICS OF JAMES JOYCE

Prolegomena

.

JOYCE's obsession with his own image is self-evident and well-illustrated not only by biographical facts but also, most emphatically, in his works.[1] He is not content to use material derived from experience; he insists on placing an image of himself at the heart of his books. Most spectacular in this respect is *Stephen Hero,* in which Stephen is clearly presented at the prototype of the artist in the romantic tradition, the masterful, all-embracing, though virtually outcast, genius. The tendency is no less perceptible with the treatment of the artist in such early critical productions as "Ibsen's New Drama" or "The Day of the Rabblement." The attitude tallies with a genuine, though youthful, admiration (if not fascination) for Byron and, just as characteristically, for Shelley, who guided his first steps as critic. But that, no less than his admiration for Wordsworth, is not enough to sum up his position as that of a belated romantic. Two or three generations had passed, and several intellectual revolutions had taken place. We shall soon realize how genuinely Joyce was a child of his age—in his style, in his general outlook, in his specific approach to modern literature.

Indeed, the very word *literature* is a case in point. The word recurs time and again in the reminiscences of Joyce by his contemporaries. When reviewing *Chamber Music* in the *Freeman's Journal,* his friend Thomas Kettle observed that "those who remember University College life of five years back will have many memories of Mr. Joyce. Wilful, fastidious, a lover of elfish paradoxes, he was to the men of his time the very voice and embodiment of the literary spirit."[2] And Constantine Curran insists that "what distinguished him most was not the exceptional character of his reading, or the maturity of his own mind, but his complete absorption in the art and function of literature."[3]

"The art and function of literature": Joyce seemed intent not so much on being a man of letters as on assessing literature, what it meant, the goals it might set itself, the values it embodied, the trap it should try to avoid. Hence his rather hesitant use, at least in his early texts, of such words as *littérateurs* or *man of letters,* often used by him negatively, as so often in French *fin-de-siècle* writings, but nonetheless inseparable from *literature* as suggestive of some artistic excellence and worthy of serious critical attention. Indeed, he early gained a reputation as an exacting reader, inflexible in his judgments. His exchange with C. Lewis Hind, the editor of the *Academy,* has become famous:

> "I thought . . . that I was to convey to your readers what I considered to be the artistic value of the book you gave me."
> "Precisely. That is what I want."
> "Well . . . I don't think that it has any value whatsoever, aesthetic or otherwise, and I have tried to convey that to your readers."[4]

As we know, the ensuing break with Hind did not dissuade him, at least for a time, from accepting to review some twenty books for various Dublin newspapers;[5] nor did he then prove more lenient: although Lady Gregory had shown real, active kindness to him, his review of *Poets and Dreamers* is uncompromising at times, even ironical (*CW,* 102–5). It is only fair to add that he was not more flexible with himself, as his rejection of *Stephen Hero* shows,[6] and his eventual refusal to write potboilers confirms.[7]

There are other reasons for taking Joyce at his word when he states his artistic conceptions. In the first place, and this is in direct line with what precedes, he placed his aesthetic in a carefully planned literary program, as described in a letter he wrote to his mother from Paris on 20 March 1903: "My book of songs will be published in the spring of 1907. My first comedy about five years later. My 'Aesthetic' about five years later again."[8]

The statement clearly shows that the theory in question was not conceived as derivative, an extension from some existing system or school of thought (in which case fifteen years would have been an unnecessarily long lapse of time). On the contrary, we are given to understand that his method was to follow a sort of dialectical progression in which theory was to be a phase, a major, pivotal phase, in the development of a poetic, creative practice, closely interwoven with theoretical elaboration. An aside in the diary of his brother Stanislaus, probably about the same date, provides additional evidence of his ambition: "Whether he will build up anything broad—a drama, an aesthetic treatise—I cannot say."[9] But an indication of the scope of his project is given in *Stephen Hero* when, commenting on Stephen's relationship with Maurice, Joyce writes: "On their way in every evening the heights of argument were traversed and the younger boy aided the elder bravely in the building of an entire science of aesthetic" (*SH,* 36).

These statements immediately raise the question of his relation to the "aesthetic" mood of the preceding period: to what extent does Joyce follow in the path opened by Walter Pater and his "decadent" successors? The point here is not to exploit superficial verbal or intellectual analogies or even affinities that might be discovered between the two authors in order to demonstrate some influence. Our aim is not to determine whether Joyce was Pater's disciple and successor but rather, in due course, to establish Joyce's own theoretical position, its genesis and development. In the same way, we must not fall into the trap he prepared for us, by focusing our interest on Ibsen alone, or even on a handful of exotic names on the basis of the interest he was supposed to feel for things Continental. His comparative neglect of contemporary English trends is only the negative side of a genuine absorption in a broader "tradition" to which he alludes rather cryptically time and again, and which heralded similar attitudes on the part of T. S. Eliot and Ezra Pound a full decade later.

Here again we are threatened by hasty oversimplifications

3

and may be misled. A couple red herrings are, if I may say so, a particularly bright red, one involving Thomas Aquinas more than any other. The facts of the Aquinas case are well-established. In the first place there is W. B. Yeats: "He [Joyce] thinks that everything has been settled by Thomas Aquinas, so we need not trouble about it,"[10] a statement that lends substance to the well-known pronouncement in *A Portrait of the Artist,* in which Stephen Dedalus describes "his aesthetic" as "in the main applied Aquinas," that we might otherwise feel compelled to dismiss, or at least qualify, as purely fictional. However, a couple of years later Stanislaus observed that his brother had "an exalted opinion of philosophy. He upholds Aristotle against his friends, and boasts himself an Aristotelian."[11] One question we shall have to answer is: what is the nature of the conciliation or synthesis Joyce effects of this scholastic-cum-peripatetic tradition (the combination indeed was not new)[12] with "aesthetic science"?

Joyce's Jesuit training had evidently prepared him to take full advantage of the scholastic heritage. However, Father William T. Noon, who has done a definitive study of the question, observes that Joyce's training in the field had been far from systematic.[13] Contrary to what one might believe, Joyce's masters at Belvedere College did not give him a proper grounding in scholastic philosophy. Thomism did not appear in the school curriculum or even, more surprisingly, in that of University College, St. Stephen's Green, because of its special status in relation to the state. In any case, Joyce did not attend any course in either philosophy or theology, nor was he member of the Academy of St. Thomas Aquinas, which was founded there in fall 1901. However, the very existence of such a body testifies to a general—if diffuse—interest in Thomism among students, probably under the influence of two metaphysicians, Father Joseph Darlington and Professor William Magennis, both Thomists as well as former professors of literature (a qualification that may have been decisive in drawing Joyce into their orbit). Exchanges between instructors and the then small group of students were frequent and easy, and the scene in *A Portrait of the Artist* between Stephen Dedalus and the Dean of Studies, whose model appears to have been Father Darlington, can be considered paradigmatic. Besides, Aquinas's works were of course available at the neighboring National Library (which acted as University Library for University College students), though Joyce also refers his readers to a book that was certainly easier of access on the Continent than elsewhere. It must not be forgotten, either, that Thomism was being revived in most Catholic countries at the turn of the century, following the decision of the church in 1879 to make Aquinas the cornerstone of orthodox teaching. The *Revue néo-scolastique,* which Joyce probably consulted, was founded during the last decade of the century.

Now, at a first estimate, one may feel that Joyce, for intellectual as well as personal reasons, was bound to be less at ease with pure Thomism than with speculations involving, along with it, its Aristotelian references and grounding. As Jean Jacquot[14] and Father Noon have observed, to speak of "aesthetics" in relation to Aquinas sounds incongruous. This is what Etienne Gilson says on the matter:

> Philosophies of art have been based on Saint Thomas Aquinas' doctrine. "Attributed to" would be more correct than "based on." To my knowledge, Saint Thomas has been almost silent about the arts of the Beautiful as such. No philosophy of art nor any aesthetic is to be found in his writings. You can only find elements of a calology suggested to him by Platonising Denys the Areopagite, but the metaphysics of the Beautiful is part of ontology; it extends beyond the realm of art in all respects. You can also find in it a definition of art which has wrought considerable damage, though it was not destined to define art in itself, and still less the art of the Beautiful, but rather to distinguish it from ethics.[15]

And elsewhere:

> Calology belongs to metaphysics. Its object is the beautiful as transcending Being: it is a sub-section of ontology. Being as beautiful extends far beyond the realm of art. . . . Aesthetics is the science of the experience of the Beautiful such as the fine arts give birth to it. I don't know whether this field of study is a science. . . . The proper object of a philosophy of art . . . is man's

activity as maker, the ultimate goal of which is the reproduction
of beautiful objects. . . . Those two fields of study are distinct,
just as writing a symphony is distinct from listening to it.[16]

It would seem that Joyce did not fall into the trap pointed
out by Gilson: "Because they failed to trace Saint Thomas back
to Aristotle, some great minds created, as it were *ex nihilo
thomismi,* an aesthetic that they placed under his authority."[17]

The trap was easier for Joyce to avoid because his very aca-
demic training was largely along those lines. Constantine Curran says about the first lecture in the English Literature course:
"The lecturer was Father Darlington and his first words were
from Aristotle's *Poetics.*" Another friend, Felix Hackett, is even
more specific:

> The University atmosphere around 26 St Stephen's Green (Uni-
> versity College) was [. . .] peripatetic [. . .] in the philosoph-
> ical sense, as is evident from the description given by Joyce in *A
> Portrait of the Artist as a Young Man.* The aesthetic discussion
> with Father Darlington may be an idealized or a synthetic ver-
> sion of many such talks, but it conveys the essence of the spirit
> of reference to Aristotle which was the salient characteristic of
> Father Darlington's interventions in the discussions of the L H
> [Literary and Historical] and other societies.[18]

Herbert Gorman's biography, written very much under
Joyce's influence, confirms that "his readings or rather reread-
ings in Aristotle were but a continuance of the road he had naturally found and followed under Jesuitical direction."[19]

•

I HAVE said enough for the moment of a tradition that I shall
discuss in greater detail with specific reference to Joyce's notes.
What requires examination now is how—if not yet why—Joyce
redirects this tradition along more personal lines. We may be
helped at this point by a statement from his earliest autobio-
graphical sketch, "A Portrait of the Artist," written in early
1904 for the newly founded Dublin magazine *Dana,* whose
editor eventually refused it. The general tone, though flamboy-
ant, is one of spontaneity (it was in fact written over a week-

end) and sincerity. Joyce says simply of his subject: "He had interpreted for orthodox Greek scholarship the living doctrine of the *Poetics*."[20] "Interpreted" and "living" strangely echo "applied" in "applied Aquinas" and add another dimension to it. The words suggest both a historical perspective of impermanence and decay compensated for by rebirth and the necessity to reread ("interpret") the text of past doctrine: a dialectic that the use of the word "applied" tends to specify as Hegelian, in the spirit if not in orthodox doctrinal terms.

Indeed, one major intellectual trend of the time was neo-Hegelian. As Anthony Ward points out,[21] from the publication of James Hutchinson Stirling's *The Secret of Hegel* in 1865 and until the end of the century, Hegel's philosophy was the major influence in English philosophy. His *Logic*, which occupies a dominant position in his system, was translated and commented upon at Oxford by William Wallace as early as 1874, and it was reprinted several times. Translations of his "Philosophy of Art" appeared first in the United States in 1879,[22] and then in England.[23] The last decade of the century is literally crowded with translations: *The History of Philosophy* (by Haldane and Simpson, 1892), *The Philosophy of Mind* (by W. Wallace, 1894), *The Philosophy of Religion* (by Speirs and Sanderson, 1895), *The Philosophy of Law* (by S. W. Dyde, 1896), and so forth. All these translations reflect the widespread interest in Hegel that English philosophers such as T. H. Green and Bernard Bosanquet aroused among intellectuals. This influence had quite perceptibly percolated through the works of Walter Pater, as Anthony Ward has demonstrated. It must be admitted, in fairness, that some of these books are covertly derivative, or influenced by the translator's own philosophy rather than strictly faithful to the original. Such is the case of the Hastie volume, a short (120 page) compendium of Hegel's philosophy of art made up of two digests, one by Hastie, the other by Michelet (not Jules, but C. L., of whom the "Introduction" says, however, that "no man living is in such essential union with the spirit of Hegel, nor has anyone a better right to speak for the master"). The fact that Hegel's *Aesthetics* was not published in his lifetime, but was compiled in later years out of lecture notes, certainly lent his doctrine an unusual flexibility and created the occasion of abundant intellectual exchanges as well as distortions.

Bernard Bosanquet is a good example of this effect. His partial translation of Hegel's *Philosophy of Fine Art* was published as early as 1887,[24] and his *A History of Aesthetic* five years later.[25] As may be expected in view of his philosophical leanings, the latter book is not a mere catalogue of aesthetic doctrines through the ages, but actually a dialectical history of aesthetic consciousness[26] winding up with an examination of the requirements of modern aesthetic science and of the perspectives open to modern art. In this connection, other contemporary developments, less systematic and more limited in scope, are well worth mentioning, as they complement Bosanquet's project and simultaneously profit by its suggestions. Such is the case with S. H. Butcher's critical edition of Aristotle's *Poetics,* first published in 1895,[27] in the light of which Bosanquet perceptibly modified his account of Aristotle. Conversely, Butcher, in whose book Hegelian influences can be discerned,[28] revised his text as early as the second edition (1897), with a "Preface" explicitly acknowledging his debt to Bosanquet.[29]

Such a statement of Butcher's as Aristotle's "philosophy has in it the germs of so much modern thought, that we may almost without knowing it find ourselves putting into his mouth not his own language but that of Hegel"[30] provides an interesting background to Joyce's statement about "the living doctrine of the Poetics." Butcher and Bosanquet were making exciting intellectual news exactly at the time when Joyce was being exposed to the Aristotelian teaching of his English Literature professors. We can only speculate inconclusively on whether the latter directed him to them, or whether his private readings triggered his project. What is certain is that they were part and parcel of the contemporary cultural scene and closest to Joyce's preoccupations. They could not but open to him areas of investigation all the more exciting as they were adventurous. At the end of his *A History of Aesthetic,* Bosanquet had solemnly warned: "The soul has won its intellectual liberty, and with it an infinite capacity for making mistakes, and this it will never surrender."[31] Stephen Dedalus seems merely to echo him, not only in *A Portrait of the Artist* ("I am not afraid to make a mistake, even a great mistake, a life-long mistake and perhaps as long as eternity too," *PA*, 247), but also as late as *Ulysses:* "A man of genius makes no mistake. His errors are volitional and are the portals of discovery" (*U*, 190).

"Mistakes," "errors": Joyce is giving us here the right context of his research, and probably something more. His definition of the epiphany is well known, although it was meant to remain concealed in the unpublished manuscript of *Stephen Hero:* "By an epiphany [Stephen] meant a sudden spiritual manifestation, whether in the vulgarity of speech or of gesture or in a memorable phase of the mind itself" (*SH*, 211). I shall refrain at this point from commenting on Joyce's choice of the word, on its etymology and cultural connotations, for, as is well known, his definition develops into a systematic aesthetic exposition that is of chief concern. However, it is worthwhile to examine how it crops up, as it were incidentally, out of a narration of the conflict between himself and his family, and especially his mother, a conflict that, again, connects with his own ambiguities and uncertainties: on the one hand, "he had come to the conclusion that nature had designed him for a man of letters and therefore he determined that, in spite of all influences he would do as nature counselled" (*SH*, 208), on the other hand, he insisted on "working out the enigma of his position in his own way" (*SH*, 209), and gradually drifts from a tense dialogue with his mother to a fierce criticism of women in general and of one Emma in particular. The final touch to his (senti)mental confusion comes when the writer distances himself from the scene by granting that "it did not really strike [Stephen] that the attitude of women towards holy things really implied a more genuine emancipation than his own" (*SH*, 210). "Working out the enigma of his position" is indeed the motto, and he soon comes to the logical, if inconclusive, conclusion: "He toyed also with a theory of dualism which would symbolize the twin eternities of spirit and nature in the twin eternities of male and female and even thought of explaining the audacities of his verse as symbolic allusions" (*SH*, 210). We shall revert to the epiphany after completing our general survey. Suffice it for the moment to observe that this existential background to Joyce's aesthetic and his pet concept, though palpably present, has too often been neglected. It certainly does not provide immediate, easy answers, but it adds the original, exceptional dimension we may expect of any of Joyce's endeavors.

Joyce obviously did not surrender to any one approach, and we shall soon have the occasion to point to other landmarks in his mental navigation. Let us now draw the list of the documents on which to base our own enquiry before examining, as a preliminary test, two of the early minor ones. We shall then scrutinize two groups of documents. The first one centers on the notion of drama: the "Royal Hibernian Academy 'Ecce Homo'" paper of 1899, and "Drama and Life," a lecture delivered to the Literary and Historical Society of University College, Dublin, in 1900. The other one sums up Joyce's shift of interest to Ibsen, then away from him: "Ibsen's New Drama," an article published in the *Fortnightly Review* in April 1900, and "The Day of the Rabblement," a pamphlet published in 1901. "James Clarence Mangan," a 1902 lecture of great significance, shall be examined by itself. It is only after following Joyce thus far that we shall turn to the "aesthetic," theoretical fragments proper, the Paris Notebook and the Pola Notebook, complete with Joyce's "Notes from Aristotle."

CHAPTER ONE

Explorations

.

BECAUSE Joyce does not seem to have kept a diary or left any kind of memoir of his adolescent years distinct from his fiction, it is difficult to determine when he began to devote serious attention to poetics or aesthetics. However, it so happens that two of his early essays, written during his Matriculation year at University College, Dublin, in 1898–99 (i.e., when he was about sixteen or seventeen), have come down to us,[1] the first in a slightly incomplete form. Although their survival may be ascribed to mere chance,[2] it is worth observing that Joyce chose to keep them in the first place; they indeed deserve close attention.

The editors of *Critical Writings* are probably wrong to suggest "Force" for the missing title of the first essay, in which the words "subjugation" and "subjugate" recur again and again.[3] Such a title is misleading, inasmuch as it emphasizes violence rather than the dominant theme of cultural regulation. As Richard Ellmann suggests, Ruskin's influence can be felt quite clearly for the worse,[4] but also more positively, in a tentative discussion of imagination in which Joyce tries to strike a balance between romantic and Ruskinian imagination:

> In works of fancy a too prolific imagination literally flys *[sic]* away with the author, and lands him in regions of loveliness unutterable, which his faculties scarcely grasp, which dazzles his senses, and defies speech, and thus his compositions are beauti-

11

ful indeed, but beautiful with the cloudiness and dream-beauty of a visionary. Such a thing as this often affects poets of high, fanciful temper, as Shelley, rendering their poetry vague and misty. When however the gift—great and wonderful—of a poetic sense, in sight and speech and feeling, has been subdued by vigilance and care and has been prevented from running to extremes, the true and superior spirit penetrates more watchfully into sublime and noble places, treading them with greater fear and greater wonder and greater reverence, and in humbleness looks up into the dim regions, now full of light, and interprets, without mysticism, for men the great things that are hidden from their eyes, in the leaves of the trees and in the flowers, to console them, to add to their worship, and to elevate their awe. This result proceeds from the subjugation of a great gift, and indeed it is so in all our possessions. We improve in strength when we husband it, in health when we are careful of it, in power of mental endurance when we do not overtax it. Otherwise in the arts, in sculpture and painting, the great incidents that engross the artist's attention would find their expression in huge shapelessness or wild daubs; and in the ear of the rapt musician, the loveliest melodies outpour themselves, madly, without time or movement, in chaotic mazes, "like sweet bells jangled, out of tune and harsh." (*CW,* 21–22)

Try to forget, if not to forgive, the almost parodic style and the schoolboyish conventionality of the message. Joyce's attack of "misty" poetry, of the "cloudiness and dream-beauty of a visionary," is obviously directed, beyond romantic literature, at the adepts of the Celtic Twilight who were holding pride of place in late-nineteenth-century Dublin. He is already trying to make room—or at least to prepare the ground—for his own guns, one of the biggest being "classicism," for which he enlists Hegel's help. Joyce's rather mild criticism of imagination is on the whole fairly close to the conception of Hegel that his contemporaries had, as Anthony Ward observes: "The directing principle of Hegel's thought as it was seen by Pater's contemporaries was the search for unity, for a principle of perception to which the differences and contradictions in experience might be reduced."[5]

Characteristically, Joyce is critical of Shelley rather than of

Coleridge, a follower of German philosophical trends, and his position is reminiscent of Walter Pater's views.[6] Indeed, "the great things that are hidden . . . in the leaves of the trees and in the flowers" seems but a commentary on the Hegelian conception of nature as presented, for instance, by William Wallace: "A Philosophy of Nature is only half a philosophy. Its purport is to set free the spirit in nature, to release intelligence from its imprisonment in material encasements which hide it from the ordinary view, and to gather together the *disjecta membra* of the divine into the outlines of one continuous organization."[7]

So, on closer examination, we can say that Joyce, after discarding art that confines "the unutterable" and "defies speech," presents the poet once more as an "interpreter," and generally opens the perspective of mediation. His criticisms of impatience, of "the fretful temper," and of "melodies that outpour themselves, madly, without time or movement, in chaotic mazes," prefigure his praise of classicism in "James Clarence Mangan." Indeed, one of the best commentaries on his approach may be found in this passage from Hegel's *Aesthetic:* "While symbolic art is unceasingly tossed about from one form to another without succeeding in settling on a more or less adequate one, while the artist gives free play to his unbridled imagination, in order to adjust to his meaning a variety of forms, each of which proves to be inadequate, the classical artist . . . forces upon himself limitations and measure."[8]

The introduction of this reference to classicism helps underscore the point that Joyce is careful to dissociate "force," or violent subjugation, from what I have described as "cultural regulation." For his perspective is definitely historical and cultural: "a man's history of progress" (*CW*, 20); "the coming of man on his onward way" (*CW*, 22). His conception of subjugation is strikingly consonant with what modern structuralist thought describes as "symbolic law," prohibition, or the interdict and consequent mediation. Such is the spirit of his conclusion:

> [Subjugation] is an innate part of human nature, responsible, in a great way, for man's place. Politically it is a dominant factor and

a potent power in the issues of nations. Among the faculties of men it is a great influence, and forms part of the world's laws, unalterable and for ever—subjugation with the existence also of freedom, and even, within its sight, that there may be constant manifestation of powers over all, bringing all things under sway, with fixed limits and laws and in equal regulation. (CW, 24)

"The Study of Languages" (CW, 25–30) further illustrates Joyce's involvement in serious aesthetic speculation. The editors of the *Critical Writings* date this essay from the same year. It obviously echoes personal interests, because at that time he was making his choice of Italian as his special subject at University College, and the language question was a consuming topic of discussion among Dublin intellectuals.[9] For writers, the question boiled down to this: should Irish literature be written in English or in Gaelic? Joyce took sides fairly quickly and, after attending a course in Gaelic at the university, gave it up "because Patrick Pearse, the instructor, found it necessary to exalt Irish by denigrating English, and in particular denounced the word 'thunder'—a favorite of Joyce's—as an example of verbal inadequacy."[10]

The essay is typical in other ways, too. In the first place it testifies to Joyce's attentive and retentive reading of Ruskin's works, as the opening paragraph shows:

In the church of San'Maria Novella there are seven figures by Memmi, named the seven earthly Sciences. Reading from right to left, the first is the "Art of Letters" and the seventh "Arithmetic." The first is oftener called Grammar because it refers more directly to that branch of "Letters." Now the artist's idea in this arrangement was to shew the gradual progress from Science to Science, from Grammar to Rhetoric, from Rhetoric to Music and so on to Arithmetic. In selecting his subjects he assumes two things. First he assumes that the primary science is Grammar, that is, that science which is the first and most natural one to man, and also that Arithmetic is the last, not exactly as the culmination of the other six, but rather as the final, numbered expression of man's life. Secondly, or perhaps first, he assumes that Grammar, or Letters, is a science. His first assumption classes, if it does nothing more, Grammar and Arithmetic together as the first and the last things in human knowledge. His second as-

14

sumption, as we have said, makes Grammar a science. Both of these assumptions are directly opposed to the opinions of many illustrious followers of Arithmetic, who deny that Letters is a science. (*CW,* 25–26)

The reference to Memmi's picture is obviously borrowed from Ruskin's minute description of it in *Mornings in Florence.* The first, general presentation is found in "The Fourth Morning: The Vaulted Book."[11] A more detailed analysis is made in "The Fifth Morning: The Straight Gate."[12] Plate 36 offers a reproduction of the fresco between pages 378 and 379. Joyce seems to be writing from memory: he wrongly places Music right after Rhetoric, thus omitting (unwittingly?) Logic as represented by Aristotle! It is worth observing that the Seven Earthly Sciences and the Seven Heavenly Sciences are dominated by Saint Thomas Aquinas, beneath whom are the three heretics that Joyce was later to mention in *Ulysses.*[13]

For the time being, Joyce was using Ruskin rhetorically, as a mere stepping stone. The actual interest of the essay lies elsewhere. Memmi's picture, a vivid example of the uses to which medieval and Renaissance mnemotechnics can be put,[14] allows Joyce to formulate the ambition he entertains for Letters: its status as the *primary science.* Now his implacably logical mind develops the connection he has been careful to establish between Grammar and Mathematics: "The Grammar of a language, its orthography and etymology . . . are studies in the same manner as tables in Arithmetic" (*CW,* 27). Most significantly, he wishes to establish a veritable mathematical paradigm subsuming the two sciences under a common reference to Beauty: "As Mathematics and the Science of Numbers partake of the nature of that beauty which is omnipresent, which is expressed, almost noiselessly, in the order and symmetry of Mathematics, as in the charms of literature; so does Literature in turn share in the neatness and regularity of Mathematics" (*CW,* 26).

The reference to Beauty at this point enables us to trace Joyce's demonstration to its source in Bernard Bosanquet's *A History of Aesthetic,* in which Aristotle's *Metaphysics* is quoted to good effect:

15

Since the good and the beautiful are different (for the former is always a property of action, but the latter extends to objects free from motion), those are mistaken who affirm that the mathematical sciences say nothing of beauty and goodness. For they most especially discern and demonstrate the facts and definitions relating to them; for if they demonstrate the facts and definitions relating to them, though without naming the qualities in question, that is not keeping silence about them. The main species (elements? *eide*) of beauty are order, symmetry, definite limitation, and these are the chief properties that the mathematical sciences draw attention to.[15]

Bosanquet goes on: "It is worthwhile to observe that almost all the actual material of Aristotle's thought, as distinct from the method of his treatment, may, as in this case, be discovered in Plato. The principle of goodness has reduced itself to the law of beauty. For measure and proportion always pass into beauty and excellence."[16] Joyce had seized upon, and was testing, a practical application of one of Bosanquet's major operative themes, one that we shall meet again later.

Another important aspect of this essay on language is its emphasis on the historical perspective:

Something is to be said about the study of languages and there chiefly in the study of our own. First in the history of words there is much that indicates the history of men, and in comparing the speech of today with that of years ago, we have a useful illustration of the effect of external influences on the very words of a race. Sometimes, they have changed greatly in meaning, as the word "villain," because of customs now extinct,[17] and sometimes the advent of an overcoming power may be attested by the crippled diction, or by the complete disuse of the original tongue, save in solitary, dear phrases, spontaneous in grief or gladness. (*CW,* 28)

Almost immediately, Joyce insists on the crucial importance in the study of languages of the names, "venerable names," those of the "masters of English," "landmarks in the transition of a language":[18] "The careful study of the language used by these men is almost the only way to gain a thorough knowledge of the power and dignity, that are in the elements of language, and further to understand, as far as nature allows, the feelings of great writers, to enter into their hearts and spirits, to be admitted, by privilege, into the privacy of their proper thoughts" (*CW*, 29).

In *Stephen Hero,* Joyce will content himself with rephrasing the idea: "Words . . . have a certain value in the literary tradition and a certain value in the market-place—a debased value. Words are simply receptacles for human thought: in the literary tradition they receive more valuable thoughts than they receive in the market-place" (*SH*, 27).

Joyce's assertions are part of a much broader vindication of language, "poetry and imagination," as the repository of the ultimate values of humanity, of *Truth as distinct from Science:*

> Are our libraries to contain only works of Science? Are Bacon and Newton to monopolize our shelves? and no place be found for Shakespeare and Milton? Theology is a Science, yet will either Catholic or Anglican, however profound and learned, taboo poetry from their studies, and the one banish a living, constant element of his Church and the other forbid "The Christian Year"? The higher grades of language, style, syntax, poetry, oratory, rhetoric, are again the champions and exponents, in what way soever, of Truth. So in the figure of Rhetoric in Santa Maria's church Truth is seen reflected in a Mirror. (*CW*, 27–28)

Joyce's attitude is perfectly in line with Ernest Renan's in *L'Avenir de la science,*[19] especially in his praise of philology in chapter 8: "The end of philology does not reside in itself: it is valuable only as a necessary precondition of the history of the human mind. . . . Philology is the exact science of spiritual realities. It is to the sciences of man what physics and chemistry are to the philosophical sciences of bodies." It should be dissociated from philosophy; and their cooperation should characterize intellectual endeavor in modern times and constitute "true philosophy, the science of humanity": "the science of a being (man) who is in a perpetual becoming can only be his history," itself made possible only by philology and the rediscovery of literatures of all ages and cultures. For "the emergence [of philology] is not indicative of the death of literatures, as has often been said; it testifies only to the fact that their life is accomplished." Renan's conclusion is sweeping: "To criticize is to set up oneself as a spectator and a judge amid the variety of things; now *philology is the interpreter of things,* the way to communicate with them and to understand their language. Should philology perish, criticism would perish along with it, barbarism would revive, the reign of credulity over the whole world would be re-established."

Putting Joyce's discourse in a broader perspective, we must advance beyond mere individual influences and examine more closely the actual historical situation. Michel Foucault has elucidated the connection between the birth and development of philology and the emergence of literature in the nineteenth century:

> The last of the compensations for the demotion of language, the most important, and also the most unexpected, is the appearance of literature, of literature as such—for there has of course existed in the Western world, since Dante, since Homer, a form of language that we now call "literature." But the word is of recent date, as is also, in our culture, the isolation of a particular language whose peculiar mode of being is "literary." This is because at the beginning of the nineteenth century, at a time when language was burying itself within its own density as an object and allowing itself to be traversed through and through, by knowledge, it was also reconstituting itself elsewhere, in an independent form, difficult of access, folded back upon the enigma of its own origin and existing wholly in reference to the pure act of writing. Literature is the contestation of philology (of which it is nevertheless the twin figure): it leads language back from grammar to the naked power of speech, and there it encounters the untamed, imperious being of words.[20]

The Oxford English Dictionary indeed confirms Foucault's analysis in relation to English. If we leave out of account the "now rare and obsolescent" sense ("Acquaintance with 'letters' or books; polite, or humane learning; literary culture"), we observe that sense (2), though relatively modern (the first instance is dated 1779), itself restricts "literature" to the domain of a professional production: "Literary work or production; the activity or profession of a man of letters; the realm of letters." A definite departure occurs with sense (3): "Literary production as a whole; the body of writings produced in a particular country or period, or in the world in general. Now also in a more restricted sense, applied to writing which has claim to consideration on the ground of beauty of form or emotional effect. This sense of recent emergence both in English and French." The first instance is dated 1812.

This definition acknowledges a broadening of perspectives, first in space and time: it connects literary production with individual cultures and their history as well as opening the question of (world) culture as such. More remarkably still, beside this collective perspective, it opens up an anthropological and ethical viewpoint by highlighting the relation of man to Beauty and to his own emotions: a perspective of a critical and epistemological nature in the line of Kant. The vital intrication of philology and culture/literature is well illustrated by the Grimm brothers, with their dual interest in the laws of language and in the literary relics of the oral tradition of their country, in which they were confident to find something like its truthful origin.

Two or three generations later Joyce found himself in a similar predicament, though with a difference—or rather several differences—not only because the sciences of man had made considerable headway, but also insofar as to him, as an Irishman, both language and culture were problematical. To the Grimm brothers the search was a matter of historical identity. But to Joyce History, historical research of a high order, whether in the field of language or of culture, seemed doomed from the outset because, far from being woven into a mutual process of integration and appropriation, both had demonstrably for centuries been the objects of constant dispossession and disintegration: hence its nightmarish—rather than visionary— quality. From such circumstances could not but follow a concept of literature more exalted than Foucault is suggesting. Its becomes a contestation not only of philology but also of cultural history and of attendant ideology. When literature asserts "the naked power of speech," it is with the full weight and force that the Creational Word suggests; when it "encounters the untamed, imperious being of words," it is carried along with their ontological implications.

In other words, what characterizes Joyce's untenable position is that he is forced to confront at its very root the contradiction between Science and Truth. He does not feel wholly committed either to the one or to the other, but bound in obedience to them both and torn between divided loyalties. This is a pattern that became maddening as it kept repeating itself in every aspect of his life: in school and in society and most emphatically in his home, where patriarchal voices were reverberating from school and university. Stanislaus detected this inner contradiction of his very early: "Whatever method there is in Jim's life is highly unscientific, yet in theory he approves only of the scientific method. . . . The word 'scientific' is always a word of praise in his mouth . . . Jim boasts of being modern."[21]

Joyce's juvenile essays deserve more attention than we might expect. They give us the occasion to discern some of the epistemological landmarks destined to chart his intellectual course in the years following. His confrontation with the clashing claims of Science and Truth have just been emphasized. He was not the first nineteenth-century author to have been faced with them. Only his situation as an Irish Catholic was quite different from that of the post-Darwinian Protestant Victorian. Far from being ready to sacrifice literature, Joyce wished to vindicate Letters as a locus of reconciliation for Science and Truth. A scientific model, perhaps even a mathematical one, seems to haunt him. Tabulation might be a word for it, as is suggested in his comparison of Grammar and Arithmetic. In his first sketch of "A Portrait of the Artist" (1904), he presents the artist as seeking "through some art, by some process as yet untabulated, to liberate from the personalized lumps of matter that which is their individuating rhythm" (*Workshop*, 60). Tabulation, computation, the *extraction* of an intelligible structure (or rhythm) from the formless, the nonsensical, the accidental, the trivial is one aspect of the epiphanic operation.

Dimitri Ivanovitch Mendeliev had recently—in 1869—proposed an interesting type of tabulation, one that provided the framework for discoveries: it not only conciliated the unknown and the known but also meaningfully articulated them in a prospective arrangement, suggesting a scientific prophecy of sorts. It created for sublunary bodies a framework and a procedure that had so far been established only for heavenly bodies, including comets. This combination of the visual and the logical as a symbolic inscription of the experimental is a superficially at least evocative of the traditional conception of a synopsis, inherited from the mechanism of the *Ars Memoriae*. Indeed, Joyce may well have been attracted by the persistence of such a method in his time, because his only bibliographical reference (before *Ulysses*) to Aquinas is to a *Synopsis Philosophiae Scholasticae Ad Mentem Divi Thomae,* which provided a full visual exposition of Thomistic doctrine, complete with objections and answers. Fascination here is of the essence and understandable: by displaying to the mind's eye full knowledge of divine as well as secular questions, little room is left for the mortal subject, who can only immerse himself and lose himself in it. This is precisely what Joyce refrained from doing, and he does not seem actually to have used the *Synopsis*. For modern science was offering an alternative by creating not a mimetic repetition, a visual reproduction and extension of the Tables of the Law, to be obeyed or rejected in whole, but the Law of the Table, in which event and structure are constantly being (re)articulated by the subject, thus given the freedom, as well as responsibility, of *naming the new body,* of assigning to it *its identifying letters, its cipher,* which become in a sense his own—in short, a symbolic process in which the Law of the Signifier is symmetrical to the responsible freedom of the subject.

Such a freedom was no easy burden. It can be argued that Joyce's aesthetic is to some extent directed by the problem of the artist's autonomy, not so much from his social environment (as is commonly believed after a superficial reading of *Stephen Hero* and *A Portrait of the Artist*) as from possible alienation into the interpretative symbolic framework in which he had been brought up, which had shaped—and threatened to paralyze—him. The latent questions are: How can the writer's experience be symbolized by him, in his own ethical act as writer? How can the image be his own without ceasing to be symbolic? In the aesthetic discussion in *A Portrait of the Artist,* Stephen uses the phrase "his image" (when his earlier formulation had been "the image") in a most ambiguous way, leaving the reader free to understand that he alludes to his own image, not simply to any image he meets or creates; an ambiguity that, whether or not deliberate, is significant. Joyce, as Stephen, will be led to examine critical and aesthetic literature in order to find out about the dichotomy between image and symbol, which will lead him deep into theology or, as he characteristically says, the *science* of theology. He wished to conciliate a certain visual experience, as quite consonant with a scientific, especially experimental outlook, with the other, ontological perspective of Being as Otherness: the epiphanic experience being where the two aspects met, enigmatically. What his account neglects is *writing as act,* the ethical dimension (remember Etienne Gilson's observation) that remains implicit, veiled, in his very narrative of the experience:

> He was passing through Eccles' St one evening, one misty evening, with all these thoughts [i.e. mother and priest, Emma, spirit and nature, male and female] dancing the dance of unrest in his brain when a trivial incident set him composing some ardent verses which he entitled a "Vilanelle of the Temptress." A young lady was standing on the steps of one of those brown brick houses which seem the very incarnation of Irish paralysis. A young gentleman was leaning on the rusty railings of the area. Stephen as he passed on his quest heard the following fragment of colloquy out of which he received an impression keen enough to afflict his sensitiveness very severely.
> The Young Lady—(drawling discreetly) . . . O, yes . . . I was . . . at the . . . cha . . . pel . . .
> The Young Gentleman—(inaudibly) . . . I . . . (again inaudibly) . . . I . . .
> The Young Lady—(softly) . . . O . . . but you're . . . ve . . . ry . . . wick . . . ed . . . (*SH,* 211)

Stephen's imperious desire to redistribute signifiers through a poetic gesture is immediately repressed and concealed by a historical, linear narrative, and the ethical quality of the experience is translated into moralistic precept: "It was for the man of letters to record these epiphanies with extreme care" (*SH*, 211). The Tables of the Law have once more displaced, replaced the law of the poet's tablets. Such is the attitude, at least, in such early effort at theorization. But Joyce was not unaware of the fascination at work in visual experience of any sort, of the traps of the scopic drive, and tried to analyze it. In a book review of "Mr Mason's Novels," he observes:

> These novels, much as they differ in their subjects and styles, are curiously illustrative of the truth of one of Leonardo's observations. Leonardo, exploring the dark recesses of consciousness in the interests of some semi-pantheistic psychology, has noted the tendency of the mind to impress its own likeness upon that which it creates.[22] It is because of this tendency, he says, that many painters have cast as it were a reflection of themselves over the portraits of others. (*CW,* 130)

Such a statement makes it plain that what brings together Joyce and Leonardo is a common interest in "the dark recesses of consciousness" and a common desire not to reject them but, on the contrary, to welcome their possible contribution to a broader aesthetic philosophy, and perhaps to poetic practice. It would be artificial at this point to offer conclusions. The remarks made so far, based on "Force" and "The Study of Languages," were aimed at clarifying the outline of the concept of epiphany as well as beginning to map out Joyce's progress. Two additional observations must be offered on two decisive operations that are part and parcel of the concept. One is the absolute break occurring in the common, everyday experience of reality, a break that shatters linear historical continuity, and (re)makes History (which is what the birth of Christ actually did). The other is the presence of the Word: words, or speech, as giving or leaving access to some Other (one sees how this would apply to the dream epiphanies as well as to the arch example in *Stephen Hero*). An inevitable consequence of this is that a new concept of time is created: a *logical time* (as opposed to the linear time of History), of which Joyce discovered, or believed for a moment he had discovered, the formula, the *poetic* formula in the *dramatic* paradigm.

CHAPTER TWO

The Dramatic Idea and Beyond

·

IT WOULD certainly be absurd to present Joyce's intellectual interests as purely idiosyncratic and utterly remote from the general mood of his time and the manifestations of contemporary concerns in actual artistic productions as well as theories and manifestos. This is especially true with regard to the "dramatic" idea on which his next two pieces focus.

Best known among these currents, or crosscurrents, is the Wagnerian craze. Joyce was not the first to have "interpreted . . . the living doctrine of the *Poetics.*" Wagner also had chosen Greek tragedy as the basis for a revitalization of the modern opera.[1] In *The Birth of Tragedy,* Nietzsche had made himself an eloquent advocate of the project: not until 1886 did he try to correct the errors he claimed had been committed by his friend, in a new "Preface" and in a series of fragments later to be collected in volume form under the title *The Will to Power.* Wagner's works had raised intense and widespread interest all over Europe. In France, as early as 1861 Baudelaire had been Wagner's self-appointed herald despite—or perhaps because of—*Tannhäuser*'s failure at the Paris Opera, and there the *Revue Wagnérienne,* founded 1886, became a major intellectual influence. In England, where a critic observed in 1896 that "everybody today is Wagnerian,"[2] George Bernard Shaw published *The Perfect Wagnerite* in 1898, just when Joyce was beginning to write.

There was a time lag, however, between the Continent and the British Isles, and we must try to keep the perspective right. For instance, the Nietzsche-Wagner argument reached England as a muffled echo only: no English translation of *The Birth of Tragedy* was available until 1909. Public opinion, even in the most sophisticated circles, was inclined to consider Nietzsche a profoundly immoral and perverse author, deserving contempt rather than consideration.[3] At best he was cut down to fit into familiar intellectual systems; such is the case, for example, with his first translator, Alexander Tille, who characteristically insists on turning him into a mere Darwinian;[4] for most of Joyce's contemporaries the dominant theme is the Superman,[5] although a rather positivistic one. Curiously enough, or perhaps not so curiously, Nietzsche is associated with Max Nordau's *Degeneration*,[6] published in 1895, which soon became one of the bestsellers of the period all over Europe.

Alone, or almost alone, among established commentators, Havelock Ellis tried to present Nietzsche more objectively in a series of contributions to the *Savoy*.[7] His relatively sympathetic approach in one of the few rather advanced magazines of the time may have enlisted the attention of Joyce and mentally involved him in the debate over Symbolism inaugurated by Nietzsche's second "Preface." That the discussion gradually extended to wider and wider circles is also apparent in the fact that William Wallace, S. H. Butcher, and other intellectuals following in the post-Hegelian wake very early came to the rescue of the German philosopher.[8]

As for Wagner, there is little doubt that in Ireland, at the time Joyce was leaving Belvedere College, Wagner's influence was greater than ever among writers. This is especially true with reference to George Moore, a cousin of Edward Martyn (one of the founders of the Irish Literary Theatre) and a friend of Edouard Dujardin, who launched *La Revue Wagnérienne* in 1886 (two years before publishing in volume form *Les Lauriers sont coupes,* in which Joyce is supposed to have discovered the so-called *monologue intérieur*). As early as 1884 with *A Mummer's Wife,* then in 1886 with *Drama in Muslin,* George Moore tried to apply to the art of the novel a Wagnerian technique such as the leitmotif.[9] Under his and other writers' influence, Arthur Symons among them, W. B. Yeats was converted to Wagner,[10] whom, very much like Nietzsche, he considered as the model initiator of a national theater and whose name he invoked in his defense of the Irish National Theatre he was then trying to establish. We shall see in a moment how and why Joyce took sides in the debate.[11] Suffice it to say that the general mood of the period was far from inimical to theoretical speculations on the drama, beyond the current Irish interest in the stage, and the recent London craze of Wilde's plays, not to mention George Bernard Shaw's Ibsenite campaign, and the rise of the music hall.

·

JOYCE's first "dramatic essay," the "Royal Hibernian Academy 'Ecce Homo,'" was composed in September 1899, as he was entering University College as a regular student. What is most striking about the piece is the contrast between the subject—Michael Munkácsy's picture—and the central theoretical concept—drama—that Joyce is trying to justify through a close analysis of the canvas. Michael Lieb, alias Mihály von Munkácsy, 1844–1900, a Hungarian painter, visited Paris in 1872, then settled in Barbizon in 1874, where he came under the influence of the famous local school and of Courbet's naturalism. Indeed, Joyce not only insists on the "realistic illusion" created by the painter—on the "naturalism . . . produced on the canvas" (*CW,* 32)—which echoes the doctrine and practice of those artists but also shows himself conversant with contemporary epistemology as well as art theory. For instance, he alludes again to what he had described the preceding year as "the great Science of Vivisection"[12] when he suggests that "to paint such a crowd one must probe humanity with no scrupulous knife" (*CW,* 35). Now the concept of vivisection in art, which can be traced back through Emile Zola's *Le Roman expérimental*[13] to Claude Bernard's *Introduction à l'étude de la médecine expérimentale,* had been taken up not only by the naturalist school but also by Nietzsche in *The Case of Wagner.* Vivisection is here presented as the scientific analysis—that is, a "resolving into parts" (Skeat)—of humanity, of human nature, with special emphasis on its "living" quality: the central character is indeed "Ecce Homo," man as presented to the people, here and now, very much as HCE will later be presented in *Finnegans Wake,* not Jesus, Mary, John, legendary, almost mythical figures established in and by tradition and become images, mere objects of synthetic reproduction.

This is why, although Mary and John are not central to his topic, Joyce goes out of his way to discuss the problem of how they should be pictured:

> It would have been easy to have made Mary a Madonna and John an evangelist but the artist has chosen to make Mary a mother and John a man. I believe this treatment to be the finer and the subtler. In a moment such as when Pilate said to the Jews, Behold the man, it would be a pious error but indubitably an error to show Mary as the ancestress of the devout rapt madonnas of our churches. The depicting of these two figures in such a way in a sacred picture, is in itself a token of the highest genius. (*CW,* 36)

The remark is a direct answer to Estell M. Hurll's recent book, whose single theme is precisely the Madonna as a symbol of motherhood.[14] To move briefly outside the field of art proper, it is worth observing that Joyce's information on his topic is substantial. Leaving aside for the moment the questions raised by the Nietzschean overtones, we may note that Joyce's view of Christ as "a great teacher" and "a great social and religious reformer" (*CW,* 36) clearly echo those of Sir John Robert Seeley (1834–95), published anonymously in 1865 under the very same title. But by insisting, from the opening lines, that his major aesthetic concept is "drama," Joyce broadens his topic decisively, blending ethics with aesthetic:

> Hence the picture is primarily dramatic, not an execution of faultless forms, or a canvas reproduction of psychology. By drama I understand the interplay of passions; drama is strife, evolution, movement, in whatever way unfolded. Drama exists as an independent thing, conditioned but not controlled by its

scene. . . . However subdued the tone of passions may be, however ordered the action or commonplace the diction, if a play, or a work of music, or a picture concerns itself with the everlasting hopes, desires and hates of humanity, or deals with a symbolic presentment of our widely related nature, albeit a phase of that nature, then it is drama. (*CW,* 32)

Drama, then, is vivisection in the sense that we have just tried to suggest: not a synthetic reproduction, but an analytic presentment of passions, of what affects the soul, the psyche. But the experimental method that Joyce adumbrates is inseparable from scientific investigation: as a "*symbolic* presentment" it involves formulation into a language, into a *written* language, as any science worthy of the name should formulate its results. We see here how close Joyce seems to come to one of his contemporaries, Sigmund Freud, both being impelled by a desire to investigate their own passions in the interest of science. However, it is only fair to grant that their backgrounds were different, and Joyce's personal references deserve to be examined in greater detail. It is enough to indicate here how both point to Cartesian science (if not perhaps philosophy?), which for the first time "provided a rationale . . . for vivisection";[15] but more of this anon.

Those observations should not blind us to the fact that the extension of the concept of drama is clearly, if broadly, inspired by Hegel's *Aesthetic:*

> Drama, which constitutes, in content as well as in form, the most complete totality, must be considered as the highest phase of poetry and of art. . . . The first point to be observed upon is the purely poetic aspect of the dramatic work envisaged independently from its scenic representation. . . . Drama aims at representing human and actual actions and conditions, by making active persons speak. But dramatic action does not confine itself to the calm and simple realization of a predetermined goal; on the contrary it develops in a milieu characterized by conflicts and collisions, and is at cross-purposes with circumstances, passions, characters which confront and oppose it. . . . This poetic synthesis [of lyrical and epical modes] is conditioned by a complete

awakening of consciousness to the aims, complications, and fates of man.[16]

Joyce was obviously conscious that his use of the concept required a commentary, and he allusively takes Maurice Maeterlinck as an example: "Maeterlinck's characters may be, when subjected to the searchlight of that estimable torch, common sense, unaccountable, drifting, fate-impelled creatures—in fact, as our civilization dubs them, uncanny. But in whatever dwarfed and marionette-like manner, their passions are human, and so the exposition of them is drama" (CW, 32).

Although this statement is too allusive, Joyce here points to a major aspect of symbolic structure. What counts in such a type of play are the actual forces behind the plot, the anecdote: "le tragique quotiden," which implies that the most genuine words remain unuttered: "Side by side with the indispensable dialogue, there is almost always another seemingly superfluous one . . . that dialogue alone the soul listens to intensely. . . . What I say often counts for very little; but my presence, my soul . . . is what speaks to you at that tragical moment."[17] Maeterlinck's "théâtre statique" has also been described as "le théâtre du silence." Joyce's characteristic interest in those productions is another example of his fascination with *the Word which implies Silence* as its proper background. The Word as reverberated from the Other supposes the existence of such a truly *symbolic margin,* the precondition of genuine exchange. And his insistence in his early theorization on the static quality in art certainly owes much to Maeterlinck's suggestion, as it may also to Wagner, when the Master praises "the ever-growing eloquence of silence" in *The Music of the Future.*[18]

Joyce, however, for the moment does not press his point in so many words and keeps to the Hegelian line:

> When the word drama is . . . applied to Munkácsy, it may need perhaps an additional word of explanation. In the statuary art the first step towards drama was the separation of the feet. Before that sculpture was a copy of the body, actuated by only a nascent impulse and executed by routine. The infusion of life, or its semblance, at once brought soul into the work of the artist, vivified

THE AESTHETICS OF JAMES JOYCE

his forms and elucidated his theme. It follows naturally from the fact that the sculptor aims at producing a bronze or stone model of man, that his impulse should lead him to the portrayal of an instantaneous passion. (*CW,* 32)

The reference to the separation of the feet is doubly interesting. It is an allusion, the first in Joyce's writings, to the legendary figure through which he eventually endeavored to make a name for himself: Dedalus. And it probably indicates that he was acquainted with Johann Joachim Winckelmann's *Geschichte der Kunst des Altertums,* book 1, chapter 1, according to which "general opinion has it, Dedalus was the first entirely to separate the lower part of those Hermes and to shape it into legs," thus suggesting movement and light. The opinion, rather than general, should be given as long-established, because it is to be found in authors such as Diodorus.[19] The observation, though repeated in Hegel's *Aesthetic,*[20] is, however, omitted from Hastie's digest. What the latter nevertheless does is to shed some light on Joyce's notion of "drama" and "dramatic," which on the theoretical side—as distinct from existential motivation—appears to be a compound of Hegel's theory of dramatic poetry and of his practical application to "the formative arts" of his concept of "Spirit."

To begin with drama, it is

the highest form of art in *speech.* It combines lyrical poetry and epic poetry with its own forms, transforming the epical events into actions which take origin from the inner states of the souls of its heroes. But again, as the completest of the arts, Dramatic Poetry unites in its most perfect representations the two other modes of formative and musical art. For, on the other side, as the Greek drama, it brings the reposing Forms of the gods out of their sanctuary upon the stage, inspires them with human feeling, and involves them in the stream of passion. From this we see the applicability to the Drama of the saying in the Greek anthology: "Out of thy passions, O man, thou hast made thy gods." . . . Thus, in the Drama, all the arts harmoniously cooperate to furnish us with the highest aesthetic enjoyment.[21]

Joyce is following in Hegel's footsteps, as is apparent from his insistence on the "human" aspect and "the interplay of passions." But it is no less evident that his choice of a picture for his special subject is wholly personal and deliberate, and we can immediately grasp one of his motivations: to try and merge into so-called drama other aspects of art that are to him of vital importance. By selecting his example from one of the "formative arts," he tries to reach back to the *emergence* of the Spirit into a concrete art form and to *analyze image into symbol*. This quest for the vital origin of art in symbolic language is quite clear in his otherwise totally pointless aside on sculpture, which again can be elucidated by reference to Hegel's *Aesthetic:*

> By Architecture the inorganic world is purified, symmetrically arranged and brought into relation with the spirit; and the temple of the God as the house of his worshippers stands complete. Into this temple, the Divinity enters as *the lightning-flash of individuality* strikes into and permeates the inert material mass. Thus does the infinite spiritual form, and not a mere outward connection of symmetry, concentrate and shape the corporeal. This is the function of sculpture. That inner spirituality, to which Architecture is only able to point, is embodied by sculpture in the sensible representation of the external matter; and the two sides—the spiritual idea and the material form—are so harmonized with each other that neither of them preponderates. Sculpture thus receives the *classical* form of Art as its fundamental type. In this sphere, every form of the sensible is also an expression of the spiritual. Hence, there is no spiritual subject that can be adequately represented by Sculpture but may be made entirely visible in a corresponding *bodily* form. By Sculpture the soul is represented, through the corporeal presentation, as in its own unity and blessedness and *repose.*[22]

One remarkable fact about Joyce's essay is that, after emphasizing the Daedalean achievement, he deliberately directs us to painting, a choice that should not surprise us now that we have observed his interest in the theoretical line of *Modern Painters,* and that requires special attention from readers of his who may be puzzled by his recurrent use of the "portrait" paradigm. Let us then follow the path he has opened for us and try to find, after Hegel, though with him, the rationale of his exposition:

31

Painting employs as a medium for its content and for the plastic embodiment of that content *visibility as such* in as far as it *specialized in its own nature,* i.e. as developed into color. . . . The visibility and the rendering visible which belong to painting . . . liberate art from the *sensuous completeness in space* which attaches to material things, by restricting themselves to a plane surface.

On the other hand, the content also attains the most comprehensive specification. Whatever can find room in the human heart, as feeling, idea and purpose; whatever it is capable of shaping into *act*—all this diversity of material is capable of entering into the varied content of painting. *The whole realm of particular existence, from the highest embodiment of mind down to the most isolated object of nature, find a place here.*[23]

One of Joyce's motives in this context is to synthesize two aspects of a twofold experience: an experience of the Spirit, of the Divine, and its simultaneous affirmation of itself in a "corporeal presentation," in a "corresponding bodily form." Christ as "Ecce Homo," Christ in the paradoxical moment of his "epiphany" as man, was the ideal paradigm, one that a budding artist cum aesthetician could identify with in "a lightning-flash of individuality." Indeed, such an epiphany, we now know, was the core of Joyce's most intense experience. What should be emphasized is that the body in this context is no less a mystery than the "spirit"; it is even more of an enigma, precisely because it seems so self-evident, so much an *object,* and yet tells a long story, that of the "original" portrait of the artist, behind and beyond "his image," his "iron memorial aspect": the body as telltale, enigmatic object.[24]

A few years earlier, in an essay that Joyce found significant enough to deserve translation into Italian,[25] "The Soul of Man under Socialism," his fellow countryman Oscar Wilde had drawn a similar portrait, which contains many features of his own image and may have inspired him:

Now and then, in the course of the century, a great man of science, like Darwin; a great poet, like Keats; a fine critical spirit, like M. Renan; a supreme artist, like Flaubert, has been able to isolate himself,[26] to keep himself out of reach of the clamorous claims of others, to stand "under the shelter of the wall," as Plato puts it, and so realize the perfection of what was in him, to his own incomparable gain, and to the incomparable and lasting gain of the whole world. . . . And so he who would lead a Christlike life is he who is perfectly and absolutely himself. He may be a great poet, or a great man of science; or a young student at a University, or one who watches sheep upon a moor; or a maker of dramas, like Shakespeare, or a thinker about God, like Spinoza; or a child who plays in a garden, or a fisherman who throws his net into the sea. It does not matter what he is, as long as he realizes the perfection of soul that is within him.[27]

Joyce selected for his commentary the moment in Christ's life that illustrated characteristically the possible tension between the individual artist and his community:

Had [Munkacsy] chosen to paint Christ as the Incarnate son of God, redeeming his creatures of his own admirable will, through insult and hate, it would not have been drama, it would have been Divine Law, for drama deals with man. As it is from the artist's conception, it is powerful drama, the drama of the thrice told revolt of humanity against a great teacher.

The face of Christ is a superb study of endurance, passion, I use the word in its proper sense, and dauntless will. It is plain that no thought of the crowd obtrudes itself on his mind. He seems to have nothing in common with them, save his features, which are racial. (*CW,* 36)

And again:

Munkacsy's conception is as much greater than [the public's], as an average artist is greater than an average greengrocer, but it is of the same kind, it is to pervert Wagner, the attitude of the town. Belief in the divinity of Christ is not a salient feature of secular Christendom. But occasional sympathy with the external conflict of truth and error, of right and wrong, as exemplified in the drama at Golgotha is not beyond its approval. (*CW,* 37)

Joyce's fascination with Christ's figure was an enduring one, as it appears from the 1904 "A Portrait of the Artist" ("The air of false Christ was manifestly the mask of a physical decrepitude")[28] and from the notes for what was to become *Stephen Hero.*[29] But again it is absolutely necessary to see through the

33

looking-glass portrait (*pace* Saint Paul and his First Epistle to the Corinthians) into its dramatic lineaments. Drama, as Joyce uses the word, is a concept that formulates through art complexities and contradictions that he was discovering at the vital core of his experience—complexities insofar as he indicates, after Hegel, that drama formulates human passions in words ("The Drama is the highest form of Art in speech") and through the Word; contradictions insofar as drama presents human bodies as *images* (i.e., meaning in *praesentia*) that can be analyzed into symbolic elements, or signifiers (i.e., *in absentia*). Could the Word, as symbolic speech, traverse such body images and thus convey a glimpse of Truth in relation to the Real?

.

YOUNG James Joyce's essay was only a trial run. It was dated September 1899. As early as 9 October he submitted the project of a lecture, "Drama and Life," to be delivered before the Literary and Historical Society of University College. The essay was completed by early 1900[30] and was read on the night of 20 January. Eugene Sheehy says about the event:

> The theme of the paper was high praise of Ibsen as dramatist; and most, if not all, of the speakers—including Th. Magennis, who summed up—profoundly disagreed with the views advanced by Joyce and criticized Ibsen severely on moral, religious, and artistic grounds. I read somewhere that Joyce made a *short* reply. This is certainly not accurate. Joyce spoke at considerable length, with great intensity and fluency, and without referring to a note. The College rule was that debates should end at 10 p.m.; and a bell rung by the porter in the hall was the signal that the time was up. On this night curfew was ignored, and Joyce kept on talking for at least thirty minutes. He dealt in masterly fashion with each of his critics in turn and to salvos of applause. . . . When at the end Seamus Clandillon[31] pounded him on the back and exclaimed "That was magnificent, Joyce, but you are raving mad," he probably voiced the opinion of many of those present.[32]

That "the theme of the paper was high praise of Ibsen" is grossly inaccurate, as any reader can appreciate, although the

34

objections made to it "on moral, religious and artistic grounds" were certainly real: there is no reason to differ from the editors of the *Critical Writings* when they indicate that "it appears that the President of the College, Father William Delany, read the paper in advance and objected to its indifference to ethical content in drama. Father Delany proposed that some passages be modified, but Joyce refused with so much firmness that Delany at last gave way. The interview with the President is described, no doubt with many changes, in *Stephen Hero*."[33] If Ibsen himself is not mentioned, and four of his plays are barely alluded to,[34] there was matter enough in the lecture to puzzle the audience, as Joyce deals with his topic, as we may now expect, in broad and—to his audience—unconventional manner.

Joyce does not hesitate to paraphrase long passages from his own "Royal Hibernian Academy 'Ecce Homo'" essay, only using more systematically and freely his by now familiar sources: Hegel and Bosanquet, to whom he adds Wagner and S. H. Butcher. However, his opening statements sound (innocuously enough) historical: following Hegel, he dismisses Oriental drama to concentrate on the Greek;[35] following Nietzsche,[36] he establishes the Dionysian spirit as the fountainhead of dramatic art; following Butcher,[37] he observes that "the conditions of the Attic stage suggested a syllabus of greenroom proprieties and cautions to authors, which in after ages were foolishly set up as the canons of dramatic art, in all lands," only to conclude that "Greek drama is played out. For good or for bad it has done its work, which, if wrought in gold, was not upon lasting pillars. Its revival is not of dramatic but of pedagogic significance. Even in its own camp it has been superseded" (*CW,* 39). At this point he significantly turns to a dialectical type of interpretation, suggesting that a change in the prevalent concrete conditions of dramatic art consequently gave rise to a new spirit:

> As the classical drama had been born of religion, its follower arose out of a movement in literature. In this reaction England played an important part, for it was the power of the Shakespearean clique that dealt the deathblow to the already dying drama.

Shakespeare was before all else a literary artist; humour, eloquence, a gift of seraphic music, theatrical instincts—he had a rich dower of these. The work, to which he gave such splendid impulse, was of a higher nature than that which it followed. It was far from mere drama, it was literature in dialogue. Here I must draw a line of demarcation between literature and drama.

Human society is the embodiment of changeless laws which the whimsicalities and the circumstances of men and women involve and overwrap. The realm of literature is the realm of these accidental manners and humours—a spacious realm; and the true literary artist concerns himself mainly with them. (*CW*, 39–40)

A couple of paragraphs later Joyce comments again on the superficially social function of literature: "In literature we allow conventions, for literature is a comparatively low form of art. Literature is kept alive by tonics, it flourishes through conventions in all human relations, in all actuality. . . . Let us not overbear the weak, let us treat with a tolerant smile the stale pronouncements of those matchless serio-comics—the 'littérateurs'" (*CW*, 41–42).

All in all Joyce is obviously embarrassed and hesitates to condemn literature outright. On the one hand, its realm is what he will soon describe as "the Hell of Hells"; in other words, "the obvious."[38] His use of the French term is a clear indication that he is echoing the current Symbolist revulsion expressed in the concluding line of Verlaine's "Art poétique": "Et tout le reste est littérature." On the other hand, and there lay the ambiguity, literature is associated with Shakespeare's achievement, one that any reader would have thought more representative of the highest form of *poetic* creation. Both paradox and ambiguity are clarified when we realize that Joyce here does little more than echo chapter 8 of Bosanquet's *A History of Aesthetic*, "A Comparison of Dante and Shakespeare in Respect of Some Formal Characteristics."[39] According to the author, Shakespeare, though he may be a *terminus a quo* ("he adopts a distinctly traditional dramatic form")[40] is also a *terminus ad quem*[41] because the general conditions of society have changed in the course of history, especially since the middle of the seventeenth century:

By the year 1600 the genuine productive impulse of the earlier [Italian] Renaissance had already exhausted itself everywhere but in England, where it was later felt. . . . [42] The rich and simple beauty which was rooted in the Middle Age had become a thing of the past. Mannerism and the classical Renaissance on one side, science and philosophy (Descartes was born in 1596), the Reformation, the English Revolution, industrial changes, and the spread of printed literature on the other, were rapidly making an end of the great artistic and architectural age of the modern world.[43]

This vision of modern art history accounts for Joyce's aggressiveness not only in reference to Shakespeare[44] but also in his praise of "the New School" at the expense of Corneille, Metastasio, and Calderon.[45] What "the New School" exactly means is another matter, one that Joyce is rather slow in explaining. The closest he comes to specific analysis is in his presentment of modern conditions of life, of modern society, its values and ideology:

> Shall we put life—real life—on the stage? No, says the Philistine chorus, for it will not draw. What a blend of thwarted sight and smug commercialism. Parnassus and the city Bank divide the souls of the pedlars. Life indeed nowadays is often a sad bore. Many feel like the Frenchman that they have been born too late in a world too old,[46] and their wanhope and nerveless unheroism point on ever sternly to a last nothing, a vast futility and meanwhile—a bearing of fardels. Epic savagery is rendered impossible by vigilant policing, chivalry has been killed by the fashion oracles of the boulevards. There is no clank of mail, no halo about gallantry, no hat-sweeping, no roystering! The tradition of romance are upheld only in Bohemia.[47] (*CW*, 44–45)

Joyce here is drawing on several authors: on romantic French literature for stylistic effect, and far more substantially on Bosanquet's *A History of Aesthetic,* itself indebted to Hegel,[48] and on Wagner.[49] The former, in particular, had emphasized Hegel's own insistence on establishing the Ideal in life and in action:

> It was natural considering the novelty of the attempt to break down the wall of abstraction round the Ideal, that Hegel should

devote nearly one-eighth of his entire set of lectures to the perfectly general question, not, *what* shapes it must assume in entering into concrete life, but, *how* it can enter into life at all. It is in this discussion that he points to a heroic past as the best ground for the art of individual character, being evidently impressed by the conflict of individual courage with orderly civilization depicted in different relations in *Götz von Berlichingen, Don Quixote* and the *Räuber.* In a civilized social order, for example, the punishment of crime no longer depends on individual heroism; it is not even a single action, but is broken up into parts played by separate agents—police, judge and jury, gaoler or executioner. Thus the great moral powers of society no longer reside in the breast of particular persons but in the cooperation of millions, and the latter relation is more difficult of portrayal than the former.[50]

Joyce is thus justified in claiming modern drama as a "communal art"[51] and one in which "The Folk"[52] is bound to play a prominent part, as Wagner precisely suggested it should: "Every race has made its own myths and it is in these that early drama often finds an outlet. The author of *Parsifal* has recognized this and hence his work is solid as rock. When the mythus passes over the borderline and invades the temple of worship, the possibilities of its drama have lessened considerably. Even then it struggles back to its rightful place, much to the discomfort of the stodgy congregation."[53]

The last two sentences echo Joyce's approach to drama in the "Royal Hibernian Academy 'Ecce Homo'" essay, when he was detecting a broadly conceived humanistic drama in an ostensibly religious picture: a constant, we might even say a structural position, with him, supported by indirect biographical evidence[54] as well as by direct evidence from his brother Stanislaus, to whom he is supposed to have declared:

> The Christian legend is more interesting. . . . The Mass on Good Friday seems to me a very great drama. . . . It was as a primitive religious drama that my brother valued it so highly. He understood it as a drama of a man who has a perilous mission to fulfill, which he must fulfill even though he knows beforehand that those nearest to his heart will betray him. . . . The chant and

words of Judas or Peter on Palm Sundays: *Etsi omnes scandalisati fuerint in te, ego numquam scandalisabor* moved him profoundly.[55]

Joyce's position on this point is significantly ambivalent. He is highly critical of "people [who] want the drama to befool them" (*CW,* 44), of the "plutocrat" supplied by "purveyors" with "a parody of life" (*CW,* 44), because those purveyors, such as Beerbohm Tree, "contend that men and women will always look to art as the glass wherein they may see themselves idealized" (*CW,* 44). "It is this doctrine of idealism in art which has in notable instances disfigured manly endeavor, and has also fostered a babyish instinct to dive under blankets at the mention of the bogey of realism" (*CW,* 44). And yet certain phrases of his sound like echoes of the paradigmatic Christ figure he had selected as his topic with Munkacsy's picture, "a part in a great drama" (*CW,* 45), and are proleptic of his next piece, "Ibsen's New Drama," a review of Ibsen's *When We Dead Awaken,* in which the central hero keeps reminding us of his masterpiece, "Resurrection." This ambivalence deserves closer examination.

In his comparison of Dante and Shakespeare as promoters of "modern"—as opposed to classical—aesthetic, Bosanquet was guided by the desire to

> disentangle from their words and to compare with one another *the abstract schemes* according to which these works were created. And although no such formulae exist, yet undoubtedly there is in every work of art an element of distinct intention, subject moreover, like all our conscious purpose, to *limits perfectly obvious to an onlooker though hidden from the author himself,* with regard to the species of art to which it is to belong, the sort of subject about which it is to treat, and the sort of point or significance which it is to possess.[56]

It appears that Joyce, in drawing his blueprint for what he described as "the New School," was following similar lines and, after disposing of the Shakespearian model, was trying to formulate the problem its members were facing in terms comparable to Bosanquet's treatment of Dante. Dante, indeed, was a much more acceptable paradigm, first because he had at a single blow created a new form as well as given full expression to the poet's soul,[57] and second because he was giving a satisfactory, coherent answer to the age-long question of image and meaning: "The visions of Dante's art were in the first place fantastic, being dislocated from their human context and thrown into shape in accordance with the imagination of a world beyond the grave; and secondly they were consciously and intentionally allegorical or symbolical."[58]

The lesson that Bosanquet drew from Dante was one that Joyce was ready to put into practice precisely because it echoed not only his Catholic education, but first and foremost his idiosyncrasy, soon to be theorized into the "epiphany." In both of them "the faith in a meaning is a great assistance to looking for one; and as a general rule the more a man looks for, the more he will see. *Beauty*, in short, *ceases to be a datum, and becomes a problem*. . . . Nothing that has a natural significance escapes [Dante's] eye and ear,"[59] whether in terms of sound, human speech, gesture, and so forth. Dante was giving Joyce a lesson in applied mysticism, as he himself was to proclaim in so many words.[60]

In "Drama and Life," Joyce was silently groping his way along the path opened by Dante and his likes, though now in terms of contemporary conditions. Among these was the new classical tradition made possible, after a couple of centuries of pseudoclassicism, by the "knowledge of genuine Hellenic life and art and ideas" inaugurated by Lessing, Winckelmann, and their successors—a relation that created the possibility of "a vital and profound aesthetic philosophy." It is easy to see how such a broadening and deepening of perspectives was going beyond Matthew Arnold's suggestion of a blending of the Hebraic and the Hellenic *moral traditions:* it added the artistic, creative, and truly *ethical dimension,* giving immediacy and substance to Joyce's aesthetic project of articulating theory ("the living doctrine of the *Poetics*") with concrete "mystical" figures (for instance, "Ulysses in Dublin"; i.e., as hero and Everyman). Joyce's very title, "Drama and Life," is an apt reminder of one of Bosanquet's opening statements: "The history of aesthetic theory . . . never forgets that the central matter to be elucidated

is the value of beauty for human life, no less as implied in practice than as explicitly recognized in reflection."[61] And although
his definition of drama is partly a paraphrase of the first paragraph of the "Royal Hibernian Academy 'Ecce Homo'" essay,
several departures from it are significant, even crucial, to an
understanding of his later development. Here is the new paragraph (additions in italics):

> By drama I understand the interplay of passions *to portray truth;*
> drama is strife, evolution, movement in whatever way unfolded;
> it exists, *before it takes form,* independently; it is conditioned but
> not controlled by its sense. *It might be said fantastically that as
> soon as men and women began life in the world there was above them
> and about them a spirit, of which they were dimly conscious, which
> they would have had sojourn in their midst in deeper intimacy and
> for whose truth they became seekers in after times, longing to lay
> hands upon it.* For this spirit *is as the roaming air, little susceptible
> of change, and never left their vision, shall never leave it, till the fir-
> mament is as a scroll rolled away. At times it would seem that the
> spirit had taken up his abode in this or that form—but on a sudden
> he is misused, he is gone and the abode is left idle. He is, one might
> guess, somewhat of an elfish nature, a nixie, a very Ariel. So we must
> distinguish him and his house.* An idyllic portrait, or an environ-
> ment of haystacks does not constitute a pastoral play, no more
> than rhodomontade and sermonizing build up a tragedy. Neither
> quiescence, nor vulgarity shadow forth drama. However sub-
> dued the tone of passions may be, however ordered the action or
> commonplace the diction, if a play or a work of music or a pic-
> ture *presents* [instead of "concerns"] the everlasting hopes, de-
> sires, and hates *of us* [instead of "mankind"], or deals with a
> symbolic presentment of our widely related nature, albeit a phase
> of that nature, then it is drama. [Here Joyce omits two sentences
> dealing with Maeterlinck.] *I shall not speak here of its many forms.
> In every form that was not fit for it, it made an outburst,* as when
> the first sculptor separated the feet. *Morality, mystery, ballet, pan-
> tomime, opera, all these it speedily ran through and discarded. Its
> proper form "the drama" is yet intact. "There are many candles on
> the high altar, though one fall."* (*CW,* 41)

Joyce is obviously drawing upon Hegel's description of "the
first form of art—Symbolic art, with its aspiration, its disquiet,

its mystery and its sublimity. . . . The Idea, having no other reality to express, expatiates in all these shapes [of natural phenomena], seeks itself in them in all their unrest and proportion, but nevertheless does not find them adequate to itself"[62]

In his dualistic presentation of "drama," by which term Joyce gives a concrete aesthetic, if not poetic, formulation of the Idea, and the persistency of which is guaranteed by a dialectic of spirit and form, he is clearly at pains to rescue the concept from a narrowly historical definition. Indeed, the closer we read the paragraph, the more we realize that he tries to "particularize" this spirit, to transfer its original import from the level of metaphysics to that of the individual experience, an experience that verges on pantheism: "a spirit . . . above them and about them . . . which they would have sojourn in their midst in deeper intimacy . . . our widely related nature." This approach is especially perceptible in his recurring reference to Truth, as if he were trying the establish that there lay the Real, ontological Necessity: "If you ask me what occasions drama or what is the necessity for it at all, I answer Necessity. *It is mere animal instinct applied to the mind*" (*CW,* 42–43, italics mine). *Truth* experienced by the *subject* as the *object* of an ineluctable drive (to use the Freudian-Lacanian concept) is a way of asserting the rights of this subject against narrowly deterministic historical conceptions, but with due reference to modern, experimental sciences of man.

It appears that Joyce is exploring the specific position of the artist as subject, as divided and torn by passions. The opening reference to Dionysus is not a mere topical allusion to contemporary (Nietzschean) theory or even simply to Walter Pater, but a confession and commentary on what he elsewhere insistently describes as "unrest"; for example, in *Stephen Hero* (*SH* 211). Such is the basis of the artist's appeal to the community of his fellow creatures: "The great human comedy [an explicit allusion to Balzac's epic of the modern City with additional Dantean echoes] in which each has share, gives limitless scope to the true artist" (*CW,* 45). He regrets that "men and women seldom think gravely on their own impulses towards art" (*CW,* 44) and insists on self-analysis: "The sooner we understand our true position, the better" (*CW,* 45). Hegel and Bosanquet sounded right to his ears when they pointed out that art and beauty had become problems, and Joyce obviously took them in deep earnest. Art and beauty were his life problems indeed. From these followed the next problems: *distance,* the right distance, and the right *perspective* for the subject. Ibsen was a case in point: "It is hardly possible to criticize *The Wild Duck,* for instance; one can only brood upon it as upon a personal woe" (*CW,* 42).

Distance, or rather distancing: how can one convey to others an experience the intensity of which borders on the mystical, in the sense that it suggests loss of self, if not even of being? Or, to paraphrase Bosanquet's analysis of Dante, what "practical mysticism" can one evolve? Can one evolve today, here and now? A new form, like the *Divine Comedy,* could be both personal and universal. At this point Joyce gives us several indications, a negative one to begin with. Although he is ready to accept some of Wagner's suggestions, he also insists on putting the opera as the last item on the list of superannuated dramatic forms, a judgment prefigured in an aside a couple of pages before: "the least part of Wagner—his music" (*CW,* 40); a position confirmed by Frank Budgen.[63] Characteristically, Joyce was ambivalent only about the Wagnerian use of myth.[64]

There is, however, a major, positive indication, which appears innocuously enough in his addition "the interplay of passions *to portray truth,*" which should be put side by side with "a single Rembrandt is worth a gallery full of Van Dycks" (*CW,* 44). Rembrandt here is patently selected as both a Dutch painter (with the attendant connotation of the phrase in nineteenth-century aesthetic criticism) and a *self*-portrait. The Dutch reference, which had become a cliché in Joyce's time thanks to George Eliot, can in this instance be traced back once again Bosanquet, in the pages immediately preceding his analysis of the heroic figure as "the best ground for the art of individual character":

> Hegel's treatment of the Ideal is the greatest single step that has ever been made in aesthetic. . . . It was Hegel who while maintaining its aesthetic nobility in the sense of Winckelmann, and

crediting it with the full aesthetic purity demanded but denied to it by Kant, at the same time accepted the extension and differentiations of it so as to constitute the principle and matter of art in all its phases and limits. As an illustration of the mode in which *the commonest nature* may enter into the Ideal or the beauty of art, Hegel in this discussion of its relation to nature briefly anticipates the eloquent defense of Dutch and German paintings, which forms the conclusion of the special section on painting in the third volume.[65]

Joyce's specific contribution here is typically indirect and ambiguous. By suggesting the Dutch paradigm, he prepares his final purple patch on the end of the heroic age, another Hegelian echo.[66] At the same time he suggests to the attentive reader that the new "hero" is now the artist. If to portray Truth is to portray the passions of the subject, passions that he says constitute the basis of his relation to his fellow men, then *self*-portrait is the only logical art form and the *new modern hero is the artist*. Even more specifically, the model hero is revealed to be the first artist to have infused life into the artwork, the artist to whom he alludes once more, though not by name: Dedalus.

Indeed, "Drama and Life," a continuation and development from the "Ecce Homo" essay, if read with due regard to its theoretical background and ambitions, is of major importance for an understanding of Joyce's whole enterprise. Rather than on Aristotle or Aquinas, his reflections at this stage are discovered to focus upon the science of aesthetics as mapped out (beyond even Hegel) by Alexander Gottlieb Baumgarten in his *Aesthetica,* along Cartesian lines. Bosanquet was pointing out that the earlier, Italian Renaissance had been the first step only of modern art. Science and philosophy, Descartes and the perspectives he opened, no less than the Reformation, the English Revolution, and industrial changes were creating a new concept of the subject: *the subject of science,* in that it seeks truth not in some external authority, but through individual reason, and also in that it reveals to itself and through itself to be the only certainty capable of sustaining science and its symbolic formulations. Now the basic Cartesian paradox that *certainty* could be derived only from *methodic doubt* was bound to appeal to Joyce, because it offered him "that certitude which among men he had not found,"[67] the very possibility of transcending his own "unrest"; in other words, the enigmatic passions of a divided subject. The so-called epiphanic experience he was trying to describe, and also to assume as poetic *act*, was characteristic of "a temperament ever trembling towards its ecstasy" and constantly intent on discovering, through its own symbolic practice (writing), the limits and unconscious "intentions" of his own bodily frame.[68] In that respect it is worth pointing out that Joyce's reflections coincide with the modern discovery of the subject of the unconscious by Freud, which in turn sheds retrospective light on the Cartesian moment.[69] Joyce could not rest satisfied in an agnostic attitude, in the vagueness and passivity it was bound to encourage; hence his criticism of Balzac and his followers, "a young generation which has cast away belief and precision after it, for which Balzac is a great intellect" (*CW,* 101). The real, ineluctable debate is again discovered to be between Science and Truth.

CHAPTER THREE

Ibsen: Hail and Farewell

.

"Ibsen's New Drama"

IN "Drama and Life" Joyce, by selecting several of Ibsen's plays for special commendation, had clearly indicated his personal preferences. Direct as well as indirect biographical evidence has established the lifelong prominence of the Norwegian dramatist in his personal pantheon.[1] But although Joyce chose to conclude his paper on a flourish from *Pillars of Society,* his scope was broad and his mentions were rather of "the New School," by which were meant Hermann Sudermann, Haddon Chambers (more surprisingly), and Wagner (ambiguously), rather than of Ibsen. The discrepancy is more apparent than real: both papers were practically prepared in the same months. Indeed, the story of "Ibsen's New Drama" is one of the best established episodes in Joyce's early career. According to the editors of the *Critical Writings,* Joyce, "before he was eighteen brashly entered into correspondence with W. L. Courtney, the editor of the eminent *Fortnightly Review.* Courtney agreed to consider an article on the play, and Joyce wrote it with copious quotations from a French translation. Since William Archer's English translation was about to be published, the article was held up so that the quotations might be put into English. 'Ibsen's New Drama' appeared in the April 1900 issue of the *Fortnightly Review.*"[2]

Joyce's continued hyperbolic praise of Ibsen in later years no less than the element of personal initiative[3] are indicative of an involvement that goes deeper than the "youthful enthusiasm" of an undergraduate.[4] Nowhere is the nature of his fascination more fully perceptible than in the present article. One of its most striking features is the number and length of the quotations, a fact that is all the more surprising when we consider the special difficulty created by the translation problem. Time and again Joyce insists on the critic's impotence. Ibsen to him is the supreme artist in regard both to History ("Than these dramas . . . the long role of drama, ancient or modern, has few things better to show," *CW,* 67) and to the Idea: "In the conversion of Rubek's views as to the girl-figure in his masterpiece 'The Resurrection-Day,' there is involved an all-embracing philosophy, a deep sympathy with the cross-purposes and contradictions of life, as they may be reconcilable with a hopeful awakening—when the manyfold travail of our poor humanity may have a glorious issue" (*CW,* 66). Here again Joyce is following a dialectical, Hegelian (not to say Marxist) line of interpretation: Ibsen is presented as the last figure, or link, in a general spiritual process that is seen as reconciling the conflicting desires of the subject and of humanity at large.

In this context an interesting aspect of Joyce's article is the insistence on Ibsen's "thought," a note that opens ("It may be questioned whether any man has held so firm an empire over the thinking world in modern times. Not Rousseau; not Emerson; not Carlyle; not any of those giants," *CW,* 48) and closes ("[His plays] are so packed with thought," *CW,* 67) his argument and lends additional force to another key concept, "mastery." The notion of "master," here, obviously cannot be confined to its literary connotation of "excellent artist, head of school." Its actual value is consonant with Hegel's conception of the master-slave relationship, understood, as it should be, in terms of subjective recognition. One may say, in a sense, that the subject of "Ibsen's New Drama" is the recognition of the subject in Ibsen's *When We Dead Awaken*—in the last resort a matter of life and death whose implications extend far beyond the ostensible metaphor in the title.

The central characters, Rubek the sculptor and Irene his former model, are oriented if not dominated by the Utopia of Absolute Truth, demystified through a painful experience of treachery and untruth and ultimately realized in death at the close of the play. The untruth that lies at the heart of Rubek's marriage to Maja[5] is of veritably symbolic import, though negatively in that it is conveyed in terms of silence, that is, with reference to the Word. Although Joyce's first approach, a sort of notice for the play, is as flat as can be, he immediately hints at a more substantial message:

> Arnold Rubek and his wife, Maja, have been married for four years at the beginning of the play. Their union is, however, unhappy. Each is discontented with the other. So far as this goes, it is unimpeachable: but then it does not go very far. It does not convey even the most shadowy notion of the relations between Professor Rubek and his wife. It is a bald, clerkly version of countless, indefinable complexities. It is as though the history of a tragic life were to be written down rudely in two columns, one for the pros and the other for the cons. (*CW,* 49)

For what is at stake when Maja complains "of the deep peace that reigns about them" is "the idle[6] promises with which her husband had fed her aspirations" (*CW,* 50). Maja upbraids Arnold for being "always, always an artist": "Your tendency is to keep yourself to yourself and—think your own thoughts. And, of course, I cannot talk properly to you about your affairs. I know nothing about Art and that sort of thing. (*With an impatient gesture*) And care very little either, for that matter" (*CW,* 56). But if they tacitly agree to part, it is because Arnold also has reached conclusions as to his own position. During the years of their married life, he says, "all the talk about the artist's vocation and the artist's mission, and so forth, began to strike me as very empty and hollow and meaningless at bottom.—MAJA: Then what would you put in its place?—RUBEK: Life, Maja" (*CW,* 56). He realizes that his attitude to Maja's desire has been more damaging than could be imagined: it has been more than mere egotistical neglect and doubled back upon him, reaching, through his failure to acknowledge the

Other's desire, to the very root of his own position as Subject of Desire.

The indirection created by Rubek's closing rejoinder ("Life, Maja") is developed in the ensuing dialogue with Irene. His realization that he has missed life and must reinstate it is another way of saying that he has somehow killed it, which is what Irene tells him in so many words. We know already that she "has served Rubek as model for the central figure in his famous masterpiece 'The Resurrection Day.' Having done her work for him, she had fled in an unaccountable manner, leaving no traces behind her" (*CW,* 53). We soon learn the meaning and extent of her absence: she has been confined in a lunatic asylum and is still leading a kind of life in death in the constant company of a Sister-of-Mercy: "I was dead for many years. They came and bound me, lacing my arms together at my back. Then they lowered me into a grave-vault, with iron bars behind the loophole. And with padded walls, so that no one on the earth above could hear the grave-shrieks" (*CW,* 54). So insanity is revealed to be the direct consequence of her position as the model in the three-corner relationship of Rubek-Irene-statue—a relationship in which she has been reduced to the status of a mere object and used and manipulated as such, as if no desire had been involved in her position. That is why she now hates Rubek, "the artist who had so lightly and carelessly taken a warm-blooded body, a young human life, and worn the soul out of it—because you needed it for a work of art" (*CW,* 57). Joyce goes on:

> Rubek's transgression has indeed been great. Not merely has he possessed himself of her soul, but he has withheld from its rightful throne the child of her soul. By her child Irene means the statue. To her it seems that this statue is, in a very true and real sense, born of her. Each day as she saw it grow to its full growth under the hand of the skilful moulder, her inner sense of motherhood for it, of right over it, of love towards it, had become stronger and more confirmed.
>
> IRENE (*changing to a tone full of warmth and feeling*): But that statue in the wet, living clay, that I loved—as it rose up, a vital

49

human creature out of these raw, shapeless masses—for that was our creation, our child. Mine and yours. (*CW*, 57)

Almost certainly not for the first time Irene has become a prey to hallucination. She mistakes a statue for her child "in a very true and very real sense" and in a psychotic fit tries to stab Rubek.[7] It is remarkable that her logic becomes infectious and she draws Rubek into her disturbed mental world. Although Joyce suggests that they have been recuperated into everyday life ("the man and the woman are left together—no longer the artist and his model," *CW*, 61), "the shadow of a great change is stalking close in the morning silence": "Irene tells Arnold that she will not go back among the men and women she has left; she will not be rescued." Just as she had felt, at the moment of stabbing him, that he was dead already, she manages to convince him that their love is dead, she leads him to a love in death that represents the perfect relationship of man and woman: in Freudian-Lacanian terms, hallucinated *"jouissance"*:

> RUBEK (*throwing his arms violently around her*): Then let two of the dead—us two—for once live life to its uttermost, before we go down to our graves again. . . . All the powers of light may freely look on us—and all the powers of darkness too (*seizes her hand*)—will you then follow me, oh my grace-given bride!
> IRENE (*as though transfigured*): I will follow you, freely and gladly, my lord and master! (*CW*, 62)

Rubek has at last become a master indubitably and is recognized as such. But again the actual, ultimate Master in this context, when all is said and done, is discovered to be Death. Irene, the soothsaying lunatic, had said so much only a moment before: "The love that belongs to the life of earth—the beautiful, miraculous life of earth—the inscrutable life of earth—that is dead in both of us" (*CW*, 61). But what was then a mere metaphor is lived through and acted out in a sort of hallucination in which the acme of *jouissance* again reveals itself as the unspeakable horror of the grave. This is a crucial moment in Joyce's presentation. For his conclusion largely concentrates on Ibsen's characterization of women, in which the critic betrays his own preoccupations and conceptions:

Ibsen's knowledge of humanity is nowhere more obvious than in his portrayal of women. He amazes one by his painful introspection; he seems to know them better than they know themselves. Indeed, if one may say so of an eminently virile man, there is a curious admixture of the woman in his nature.[8] His marvelous accuracy, his faint traces of femininity, his delicacy of swift touch, are perhaps attributable to this admixture. But that he knows women is an incontrovertible fact. He appears to have sounded them to almost unfathomable depths. (*CW,* 64)

The unfathomable depth of woman's *jouissance,* its attraction and deathly quality, was Tiresias's secret and fascinated Joyce no less than T. S. Eliot.[9] The characters now proceed to enact this self-inflicted dissolution. Rubek and Irene now accomplish with their physical bodies what sculpture had been powerless to achieve.[10] The blasts of wind of the impending storm "sound like the prelude to the Resurrection Day" (*CW,* 61). It is as if Rubek had to fulfill in life what his work was supposed to mean in art. Because the only promise of life is death, superimposing life on art, confusing life or one's own, once for all, can only lead to the ultimate, quasi-psychotic silence: the white silence that envelops them when, at the end of the play, both of them are carried away by an avalanche.

The experience is indeed that of "the beautiful, [the] miraculous," with all the ambiguity that this implies. A couple of years later, in "James Clarence Mangan," Joyce will assert that "death [is] the most beautiful form of life" (*CW,* 83). His fascination with Ibsen is patently due to this perception of a common experience verging on the ontological. As Lacan says in "Kant avec Sade," "the function of beauty [consists in setting up] the ultimate barrier forbidding access to absolute horror";[11] it mercifully blinds the subject as to Truth, inscrutable Truth. In *A Portrait of the Artist,* Stephen says to Lynch: "Plato, I believe, said that beauty is the splendour of truth. I don't think that it has meaning but the true and the beautiful are akin" (*PA,* 208). *Meaning* and *kinship*—in other words, intersubjective relationships ("How can one relate to the Other?") —are indeed the *problems* upon which Ibsen and Joyce were meeting in a common negative experience, that of aphanisis, a total loss of the subject into a blindingly white field.[12] No wonder then that the meeting of Joyce with the Norwegian's dramas was such an intense experience, one however that evoked a kindred soul rather than a master to be humbly followed and imitated. Their experiences were structurally similar, opened on the same field, and basically formulated the same problematics.

"Ibsen's New Drama" helps us to understand "Drama and Life" a little better, and, indeed, such is the theme of the conclusion: "The naked drama—either the perception of a great truth, or the opening up of a great question, or a great conflict which is almost independent of the conflicting actors, and has been and is of far-reaching importance—this is what primarily rivets our attention"[13] (*CW,* 63). The example is of a work of art in which "there is involved an all-embracing philosophy," and we have commented on the (Neo-)Hegelian tone of the ensuing development. But over and above the reflexive import that Joyce discerned in Ibsen's analysis of existential relationships, we find in his text the landmarks of an adventure into the problems of Truth and Beauty, model and master, realism and symbolism, and so forth. In a sense Joyce is reverting, beyond Shakespeare and "literature," to the perspectives opened —according to Bosanquet—by Dante, as the representative of "the medieval or early modern mind,"[14] no less than as the discoverer of "a totally new species of poetic art."[15]

Stephen Hero is quite explicit:

The minds of the old Norse poet and of the perturbed young Celt met in a moment of radiant simultaneity. . . . But it was not only [the] excellence [of the dramatist] which captivated him: it was not that which he greeted gladly with an entire joyful spiritual salutation. It was the very *spirit* of Ibsen himself that was discerned moving behind the impersonal manner of the artist. (Ibsen with his profound self-knowledge, Ibsen with his haughty, disillusioned courage, Ibsen with his minute and wilful energy.) a mind of sincere and boylike bravery, of disillusioned pride, of minute and willful energy. Let the world solve itself in whatsoever fashion it pleased, let its putative Maker justify Himself by whatsoever processes seemed good to Him, one could scarcely

advance the dignity of the human attitude a step beyond this answer. Here and not in Shakespeare or Goethe was the successor
to the first poet of the Europeans, here, as only to such purpose
in Dante, a human personality had been found united with an
artistic manner which was itself almost *a natural phenomenon:*
and the spirit of the time united one more readily with the Norwegian than with the Florentine.[16]

Joyce's insistent use of "spirit" and "spiritual" is not without
echoes of Madame Blavatski and her followers, who were
blocking part of the contemporary cultural horizon. He may be
said to incorporate something of their dark, dualistic approach, but goes a long way beyond it: he describes here a miraculous, symbolic encounter with a kindred spirit in terms
that evoke his conception of the "epiphany": a "radiant" phenomenon, spiritual though natural, natural though asserting
the dignity of man confronted with the Other and the Other
World, whether it called itself madness, *"jouissance,"* or death.

"The Day of Rabblement"

"The Day of the Rabblement" was written a year and a half
later, in October 1901, in a fit of indignation at recent developments in the policy of the Irish Literary Theatre (later to become the Abbey Theatre), which had opened in May 1899
with W. B. Yeats's play *The Countess Cathleen,* to the protests,
hisses, and boos of an overconservative Irish audience. What
triggered Joyce's anger was the decision of the management to
stage Douglas Hyde's *Casadh an tSùgàin,* written in Irish, and
Yeats and Moore's *Diarmuid and Grania,* based on a well-
known Celtic legend. The pamphlet was submitted to the editor of *St. Stephen's,* the newly founded University College student magazine. The editor accepted it but it was rejected by the
clerical adviser, Father Henry Browne. Joyce, after appealing in
vain to the president of the university, convinced his friend
Francis Skeffington, who had incurred the same rebuff for the
feminist essay "A Forgotten Aspect of the University Question," to join forces with him and publish their two ostracized

essays together at their own expense—which they accordingly did in November.[17] A highly critical review of the pamphlet was published in the December issue of *St. Stephen's,* reminding its readers of Joyce's former refusal to sign the petition against *The Countess Cathleen.* However, Arthur Griffith in *The United Irishman,* without supporting Joyce's adverse views on the Irish Literary Theatre, used it as an argument against censorship in general, asking himself why Ireland was so prolific in censors: "Turnips, he pointed out, would be more useful."

The occasion and the circumstances of publication of the pamphlet invite us to examine it first from the vantage point of the cultural scene. Although Joyce begins by sounding ambivalent toward local conditions ("The Irish Literary Theatre is the latest movement of protest against the sterility and falsehood of the modern stage," *CW,* 69–70), his tone grows gradually more and more aggressive toward his fellow countrymen: "Mr. Yeats's treacherous instinct of adaptability . . . Mr. Martyn and Mr. Moore are not writers of much originality . . . Mr. Moore is really struggling in the backwash of that tide which has advanced from Flaubert through Jakobsen to D'Annunzio. . . . However frankly Mr. Moore may misquote Pater and Turgenieff to defend himself, his new impulse has no kind of relation to the future of art" (*CW,* 71). There may have been some personal spite—or simply envy—toward successful, established authors at a time when his first dramatic experiment, *A Brilliant Career,* had been dismissed by William Archer and, worse, his recent translations of two of Gerhart Hauptmann's plays, which he had hoped might be put on the program of the Irish Literary Theatre, had been brushed aside. Nevertheless, his disappointment was not all narrowly egotistical. His objection to the Irish language as a basically—or, rather, to most Irishmen practically and existentially—dead language was already manifest. His attitude toward traditional Irish themes was identical: at a time when his war cry was "Life!" he saw them as representatives of a static—that is, at best nostalgic, if not morbid and deathlike—conception of history. In short, he had clearly taken sides in the contemporary Irish debates over the "de-anglicisation" and "de-Davisisation" of Irish literature.

His Neo-Hegelian leanings made it impossible for him to conceive of history in purely nationalistic and linear terms. His whole discourse is on a different track, and again one of his key concepts is aesthetic "advance": "A nation which never advanced so far as a miracle-play affords no literary model to the artist, and he must look abroad" (*CW,* 70); "that tide which has advanced from Flaubert through Jakobsen to D'Annunzio: for two entire eras lie between *Madame Bovary* and *Il Fuoco*" (*CW,* 71); "The Irish Literary Theatre . . . has cut itself adrift from the line of advancement" (*CW,* 71). To put it another way, the cultural problem for him, rather than contemporary Irish circumstances, is "the future of art," and a concept of tradition that extends far beyond national boundaries: "Elsewhere there are men who are worthy to carry on the tradition of the old master who is dying in Christiania" (*CW,* 72). Now what is the actual significance of this stance?

Nothing could disfigure Joyce's position more profoundly than to approach it merely in terms of literary history: of literary movements, whether English or Continental, of influences, whether national or international, of genres, whether drama or the novel, and so forth. . . . Not that eminent contemporaries are neglected here. The presence of Wagner can be discerned even though his name is not explicitly mentioned: the phrase "the future of art" is most probably an allusion to *The Art-Work of the Future,* the English title of his collection of critical essays. Numerous foreign authors are mentioned or alluded to with various degrees of approval: Tolstoy, Sudermann, Björnson,[18] Giacosa,[19] Echegaray,[20] Maeterlinck,[21] Jacobsen,[22] and so forth. Most of them, however, despite the real, though temporary, interest they elicited, appear more as a squad of supporters enlisted for the occasion, whose names are flung at the heads of a supposedly backward, Philistine public, than as guiding lights for the budding theorist.

Special attention, however, must be given to Gerhart Hauptmann[23] and Gabriele D'Annunzio, whose presence is indicative of a development, if not a significant shift, in Joyce's position. The former is presented as Ibsen's inheritor: "[Ibsen] has already found his successor in the writer of *Michael Kramer,* and the third minister [Joyce himself?] will not be wanting when his hour comes" (*CW*, 72). And, as in Ibsen's case, the importance of Hauptmann seems to lie in one particular aspect of his artistic production.[24] Like the author of *The Master Builder* and *When We Dead Awaken,* Hauptmann has cast artists as protagonists of some of his plays, at least those that Joyce chose to translate, *Michael Kramer* and *Vor Sonnenaufgang.*[25] We cannot but feel that Michael Kramer, the painter and eponymous hero of the play highlighted in Joyce's conclusion, sounds like a persona of Joyce's when he insists: "Das Eigne, das Echte, Tiefe und Kräftige, das wird nur in Einsiedlerei geboren. Der Künstler ist immer der währe Einsiedler," or, "Ich könnte alles verzeihn, aber Gemeinheit verzeih' ich nicht."[26] As to the seemingly casual mention of D'Annunzio and of his novel *Il Fuoco,* it is equally significant. On the surface it seems to reveal a growing interest in the novel as genre, an interest precipitated by his recent failure with *A Brilliant Career,* just as in terms of influences, of exposure to contemporary trends, it illustrates the persistence of Joyce's fascination with Nietzschean themes. What is ultimately still more characteristic is that Joyce chooses to mention a semiautobiographical literary production centering around the figure of an artist, Stellio, and a dying master, Wagner, with a background of "epiphanic" revelation. As Umberto Eco has demonstrated, the novel is the source, if not of the concept of "epiphany," at least of its approach and lexical formulation.[27]

In other words, Joyce is less intent on fighting ambient ideologies, whether political or ethical, and their statements, themes, or injunctions, than on delineating—beyond even the obvious seduction exercised by contemporary artists, philosophers, or writers—the major aspects and conditions of his own artistic enunciation. The first condition is (self-)assertion, established in the opening lines: "No man, said the Nolan, can be a lover of the true or the good unless he abhors the multitude;[28] and the artist, though he may employ the crowd, is very careful to isolate himself. This radical principle of artistic economy, applies specially to a time of crisis, and today when the highest form of art has been just preserved by desperate sacrifices, it is strange to see the artist making terms with the rabblement" (*CW,* 69).

Joyce's protest is less political than ethical. Such is the ground of his attack on Yeats: "An aesthete has a floating will, and Mr. Yeats's treacherous instinct of adaptability . . . etc." (*CW,* 71). And such is the dominant note of his conclusion: "Until he has freed himself from the mean influences about him—sodden enthusiasm and clever insinuation and every flattering influence of vanity and low ambition—no man is an artist at all. But his true servitude is that he inherits a will broken by doubt and a soul that yields up all its hate to a caress; and the most seeming-independent are those who are the first to reassume their bonds" (*CW,* 72).

Ultimately, the artist is faced with an aporia: how can he be and remain a master, how can he escape a natural adaptation, the natural inclination to be or to remain a slave, and in the last analysis the law of nature, which tends to reduce Difference to Oneness, indifference, and death (of spirit)? This is an inherent drive and fascination of which Joyce seems once more to be fully aware and against which he takes up arms, in his assertion of the irreducible otherness of the artist. Here is the point at which dialectics and the reconciliation it engineers are dismissed, and, Nietzsche succeeding Hegel, pure, everlasting Affirmation becomes the guiding principle. In the same way, masks and the logic of their succession[29] become the landmarks of the truly ethical quest, of the true genealogy. Which leads us to the second condition of Joyce's artistic enunciation: recognition, again, not of an Ego, but of a divided Subject; that is, in relation to the Desire of the Other. This time Joyce, in the last lines of his conclusion, formulates the recognition, not illegitimately, in genealogical terms: "Elsewhere there are men who are worthy to carry on the tradition of the old master who is dying in Christiania. He has already found his successor in the writer of *Michael Kramer,* and the third minister will not be wanting when his hour comes. Even now that hour may be standing by the door" (*CW,* 72).

It would be a serious misrepresentation to understand "tradition" in terms of linear historical continuity. On the contrary, the genealogical simile presents it as essentially symbolic, implying an operative Word and a sort of "apostolic succession,"[30] that of "ministers" in duty bound to assume the highest office after and beyond the death of the Master. Death here takes on a new, different function. It is no longer the poetic, romantic theme of an artwork presenting a binary logic of life and death and developing in terms of a possible resolution, or a secularized Resurrection. It has become an essential, though veiled, coordinate of the position of the artist as artist; that is, as in a special relation to the Word: a relation both decisive and highly problematic. As Joyce will later have Stephen Dedalus say: "To live, to err, to fall, to triumph, to recreate life out of life! A wild angel had appeared to him, the angel of mortal youth and beauty, an envoy from the fair courts of life, to throw open before him in an instant of ecstasy the gates of all the ways of error and glory" (*PA,* 172).

But what if the artist does not get the genealogical recognition that founds his pretension? The pattern now is genealogical succession, in other words the question of *legitimacy:* Who is the legitimate successor? Who shall wear the crown?[31] Who is going to be *stephaneforos?*[32] Legitimate genealogy is by definition determined by the Word of the Father, whose utterance is decisive to the point of transforming a possible bastard, if so desired, into a true-born heir.

Joyce's special position at this stage, one that is illustrated in the early (1904) "A Portrait of the Artist," is characterized by his insistence on the idea of *heroism,* a notion that serves here to typify Ibsen's vision ("heroic insight," *CW,* 49; see also "What triumph there has been here and there [in Norway] is due to stubborn conviction, and every movement that has set out heroically has achieved a little" *CW,* 70), and later to characterize Giordano Bruno, with specific reference to his work *The Heroic Enthusiasts* (*CW,* 134), as well as to his life and death. The paradox of heroism, its intrication of greatness and frailty, is that the hero through his own deeds makes a name for himself, creates a symbolic lineage, and, nevertheless, at the same time, is somehow predetermined for the semidivine ascension by his very origins: he does not start from nothing, or nowhere; he is, however distantly, related to the gods. As Maurice Blanchot points out,[33] the hero will never recover from such a dramatic contradiction that leads him from achievement to more exalted achievement, with little or no indication as to what culmination he may pretend to. Characteristically, Joyce reproached the Irish Literary Theatre for its deficiency in heroic figures, which alone might have given legitimacy to the movement: it must "set out heroically" in order to "achieve a little." Such is Joyce's standpoint, the actual basis of his exposition of the "vulgarity" of the "rabblement," a denunciation that is not to be understood in terms of taste, whether social or artistic, but with due regard to its *symbolic* import. That is also why, beyond the topical and historical situation, we cannot but grasp his no less symbolic involvement as subject. In a sense, he is using the Dublin public and the Dublin literati as whipping boys for his own shortcomings. Only a year before had he failed in having his own play, *A Brilliant Career,* accepted by William Archer the master critic. Here is what Archer said about it:

> I cannot say that I think this play a success. For the stage of course—the commercial stage at any rate—it is wildly impossible—no doubt you realize that. But taking it simply as a dramatic poem, I cannot help finding the canvas too large for the subject. It narrows down in the last act into a sort of love tragedy—almost a duologue—but in order to reach that point you construct a huge fable of politics and pestilence, in which the reader—one reader at any rate—entirely loses sight of what I presume you intend for the central interest of the drama. I have been trying to read some elaborate symbolism into the second and third acts to account for their gigantic breadth of treatment, but if you had a symbolic purpose, I own it escapes me. It may be very good symbolism for all that—I own I am no great hand at reading hieroglyphics.[34]

Archer added that he was "interested and a good deal impressed, but also [...] a good deal bewildered." Stanislaus Joyce has given a bald summary of the play that suggests clearly Ibsen's influence. Archer, however, was alive to an excessively ambitious symbolic purpose ("a huge fable of politics and pestilence"), which required from the reader (he excluded from the outset any possibility of public performance!) highly sophisticated symbolic reading. Stanislaus tells us that Joyce himself "thought less of *A Brilliant Career* than Archer did, but for a different reason. Jim did not specify the reason."[35] Whatever that may have been, the blow had certainly been serious to discover that his dramatic endeavor was found to be illegible rather then eligible by even the most sympathetic as well as acute of critics (as for Stanislaus, he does not seem to have perceived much beyond the social and psychological situation). But that was not all. Joyce, we now know for certain, had experienced another, no less personal failure in his attempt to translate Hauptmann. Even had the management of the Irish Literary Theatre decided to put *Before Sunrise (Vor Sonnenaufgang)* on the stage, his translation would not have been ready, and he knew it. In short, his present aggressiveness only thinly veils dissatisfaction with himself, and a realization that the form in which he was writing was inadequate to his ambitions. He was fascinated by the dramatic idea, by drama as a structural concept. But that did not mean drama was his poetic medium (a few years later *Exiles* was to confirm and illustrate this duality). He would have to explore his actual creative experience as writer, his actual creative urge in action, as manifesting itself in the production of poems and epiphanies. Not surprisingly, his next exchange with Archer, in September 1901 (i.e., shortly before "The Day of Rabblement"), concerns his poems. But Archer appears to have been only a little less puzzled by them than by *A Brilliant Career,* and Joyce finds himself facing another failure, which leaves him with the poetic prose of the epiphanies as his only, his ultimate resort.

It is then hardly surprising to discover that this time Joyce's most articulate praises are of the poetically inclined prose fiction of W. B. Yeats and Gabriele D'Annunzio. After insisting that "The Wind among the Reeds" is "poetry of the highest order," Joyce insists that "'The Adoration of the Magi' (a story which one of the great Russians might have written) shows what Mr. Yeats can do when he breaks with the half-gods" (*CW,* 71). What D'Annunzio's *Il Fuoco* and Yeats's story have in common is both their being written as prose fiction and their treatment of a theme involving the epiphany, of which they constitute "symbolic presentments." Both writers, and to some extend Walter Pater, to whom Joyce will refer in his next essay, provided what struck him as successful examples of poetic, symbolic prose. They maintained the exigency of poetry in the medium that Neo- or Post-Hegelians claimed was characteristic of "the future of art": "the prose of thought." Such a prose actualized the dream of a presentation of the symbolic, heroic *subject*, the "glorious body" of the Word (i.e., the epiphanic experience) in discourse.

It may just be that Joyce was realizing a contradiction in his attitude. Although he had been at pains to indicate that drama was not a matter of literary genre, his models and his experiments belonged in that category, demonstrating that he had not liberated himself from the limitations he was denouncing in others: a sense of repetition, an undue, though unconscious, respect for models, whether great men or the formal conventions of literary genres. He was gradually realizing that heroism and betrayal were connected more subtly than he had thought. The heroic position, no less than the punishment of traitors, implies for the hero the very possibility of betrayal with reference to symbolic values and status—specifically self-betrayal.[36] There was a sense of possible abjection in the position. In other words, "The Day of the Rabblement," as a formulation of his aggressiveness, is a first effort at deciphering the enigma of his failures, of his own actual stumbling on the road he was trying to pave, ostensibly for others, *sub specie aeternitatis,* in the form of an aesthetic treatise. Here the ethical stance is made out clearly. For Joyce, as for Bruno and Nietzsche, weakness and servitude and betrayal are in the subject as such, as conditions of his very existence, and inseparable from his expression. The fight to be conducted is not with others, with society as a whole or individually with its members, but with the "ineluctable" Other in him ("In here it is I must kill the priest and the king," *U,* 589), in the confrontation with essential weakness, physical and moral. His essay "James Clarence Mangan" shall tell us more about this.

61

CHAPTER FOUR

"James Clarence Mangan"

·

JOYCE'S "James Clarence Mangan" lecture is of special importance because it is his second, and last, attempt at a public,
deliberate, and articulate statement of his aesthetic and philo-
sophic convictions: an importance that is confirmed by the fact
that he was to deliver it (or a slightly revised version of it)
again a few years later in Trieste.[1] According to Stanislaus
Joyce,[2] in James's estimation Mangan was one of the two Irish
poets worthy of the name (Yeats was the other), and he composed musical accompaniments for several of his poems.[3] Eugene Sheehy remembered that Joyce was fond of reciting "The
Nameless One,"[4] and, according to Oliver St. John Gogarty,
"Veil not your mirror, sweet Aline" was often recited "in order
to show . . . what a poet Mangan was."[5] But, as Stanislaus insists, Joyce's preference had deeper roots than met the ear. His
lecture "bore witness to a determined struggle to impose an
elegance of thought on the hopeless distortion of the life that
surrounded him, but it announced, too, certain purposes from
which he never receded, and certain principles that were to
guide the course of his life through much waywardness and error. . . . My brother was clearly feeling his way . . . towards the
literary tenets that were to dominate his work."[6] We should
not, then, be surprised to find a paraphrase of the lecture in
Stephen Hero, but it is there given the title "Drama and Life"
and omits Mangan altogether, which definitely raises the ques-

tion of its actual significance in the canon of Joyce as an aspect of his aesthetic project, and also as a facet of his *Weltanschauung*.[7]

Indeed, "James Clarence Mangan" is a puzzling piece in many ways, especially as a rhetorical structure. It opens with a very general introduction defining the concepts of classicism and romanticism, and more generally literature and poetry; then a long central development focuses on Mangan's life and works, which is the occasion for an incidental, cryptic definition of imagination; and a long conclusion again discusses "poetry" and "beauty," without, however, linking up with the opening pages.

The reader of Joyce's critical writings may also be surprised at his apparent departure from the line he had been following so far. There is no mention of Ibsen (although he is silently quoted in the conclusion), of other authors that had been his references, or of "drama" in general. But on second thought, the shift of his critical attention to poetry and poets is ascribable to a specific cause; namely, William Archer's recent lukewarm reception of his poetic production. However, such is not the whole story. Following close (four months) after "The Day of the Rabblement," "James Clarence Mangan" also betrays the deeper implications that we have discovered in the former pamphlet: the ambiguous position occupied by models and paradigms, and the unusual presence of enigmatic forces at work within the personality of the artist. Such appears to be the case as early as the initial statement:

It is many a day since the dispute of the classical and the romantic schools began in the quiet city of the arts, so that criticism, which has wrongly decided that the classical temper is the romantic tempter grown older, has been driven to recognize these as constant states of mind.[8] Though the dispute has been often ungentle (to say no more) and has seemed to some a dispute about names and with time has become a confused battle, each school advancing to the borders of the other and busy with internal strife, the classical school fighting the materialism which attends it, and the romantic school to preserve coherence, yet as this unrest is the condition of all achievement,[9] it is so far good, and presses slowly towards a deeper insight which will make the schools at one. (*CW,* 73–74)

Joyce's stance probably owes something to Walter Pater's "Post-Scriptum" to *Appreciations, with an Essay on Style,*[10] just as the presentation of classicism that follows may be inspired by Matthew Arnold's essay "The Study of Poetry":[11]

> The romantic school is often and grievously misinterpreted, not more by others than by his own, for that impatient temper which, as it could see no fit abode here for its ideals, chose to behold them under insensible figures, comes to disregard certain limitations, and, because these figures are blown high and low by the mind that conceived them, comes at times to regard them as feeble shadows moving aimlessly about the light, obscuring it; and the same temper, which assuredly has not grown more patient, exclaims that the light is changed to worse than shadow, to darkness even, by any method which bends upon these present things and so works upon them and fashions them that the quick intelligence may go beyond them to their meaning,[12] which is still unuttered. (*CW,* 74)

Typically, classicism and romanticism, as traditional categories of art history, are radically reexamined from what might at first sight appear as a purely psychological angle. However, Joyce's originality, lies in a presentation of the artistic "temper"—or "mind," as *Stephen Hero* has it—as of the essence of the Idea (according to Hegel) or of the "spirit" ("drama," according to "Drama and Life"). Characterized by unrest and conflict, its destiny is dialectically to reach a stable achievement, aesthetic repose. So Joyce's first step is politely to bow farewell to the romantic *Weltanschauung* and its Platonic assumptions, while emphasizing as decisive the part played by the "artistic temper" as giving utterance to "these present things," as enunciating the meaning of the Real in experience. He is rather following a Neoplatonic line, or, to be more accurate, the doctrine Bosanquet was telling him was to be found in Plotinus, according to whom "a beautiful *material* thing is produced by participation in *reason* issuing from the divine."[13] (Plotinus thus modifies and reapplies Plato's terminology: "Material beauty is still an image or a shadow, but it is an image or shadow issuing from reason, and appealing to the soul through the same power by which reason brings order into matter. . . . Therefore the whole metaphysical assumption that is limited by ordinary perception, which assumption is one with the imitative theory of fine art, is now broken through. It is henceforth understood that *art is not imitative but symbolic.*)[14] Such a doctrine enabled Joyce to conciliate an interest in "these present things" and faith in "quick intelligence" in quest of "still unuttered . . . meaning" and provided the broad perspectives of his essay.

In particular, the doctrine helps us to understand his next development:

> No error is more general than the judgment of a man of letters by the supreme laws of poetry. Verse indeed is not the only expression of rhythm, but poetry in any art transcends the mode of its expression; and to name what is less than poetry in the arts, there is need of new terms, though in one art the term "literature" may be used. Literature is the wide domain which lies between ephemeral writing and poetry (with which is philosophy), and just as the greater parts of verse is not literature, so even original writers and thinkers must often be jealously denied the most honorable title; and much of Wordsworth, and almost all of Baudelaire, is merely literature in verse and must be judged by the laws of literature. (*CW,* 75)

So Joyce now appears to have replaced his pet concept of "drama" by the tamer one of "poetry." As the context indicates, it should be taken seriously; indeed, the Hegelian derivation is obvious: "Poetry is conformable to all types of the beautiful, and extends over them all, because artistic imagination is its proper medium, and *imagination* is essential to every product that belongs to the beautiful, whatever its type may be."[15] And again: "Poetry is the universal art of the mind which has become *free in its own nature,* and which is not tied to find its realization in external sensuous matter, but expatiates exclusively in the *inner space,* and *inner time* of the ideas and feelings. Yet just in this its higher phase, art ends by transcending itself, inasmuch as it abandons the medium of a harmonious embodiment of mind in sensuous form, and passes from the poetry of imagination into the *prose of thought*."[16]

Now the very topic Joyce had chosen, a poet illustrative of an exalted conception of poetry, indicates that he insists on asserting the rights of "the poetry of imagination," while obviously exercising his intellectual gifts as a theorist in "the prose of thought." There is a double paradox here, which is more apparent than real. His inquiry bases itself patently upon a Neo-Hegelian analysis, but it polarizes itself on only two of the three types of art examined in the *Aesthetic,* the classical and the romantic. Although the symbolic principle is involved in the discussion, it is never mentioned as such. The other paradox is the presentation of the Idea, or Spirit, in psychological, or at least individualized, terms, as "tempers." These two departures from the Hegelian pattern are correlated and obey the same motive: the displacement of the dialectical process into the individual consciousness, or mind, accounts for the suspension of any reference to symbolic art and to the very concept of symbolism. Symbolism for Joyce is neither a school[17] nor a phase in the history of aesthetic consciousness; it is a principle common to all artists, which energizes their productions as constant research: as Bosanquet was pointing out in connection with the system of Scotus Erigena, "*Symbolism is a mode of interpretation;* and with all its enormous risks of arbitrariness, has the one advantage of absolute universality."[18]

Why should we reintroduce a word and a notion that Joyce had carefully avoided? Simply because it is the heart of his epistemology (as much as, if not more than, it is part and parcel of the Hegelian system). He rewrites Plato's Cave myth:[19] the romantic temper, "which as it could see no fit abode here for its ideals, chose to behold them under insensible figures, comes to disregard certain limitations, and, because these figures are blown high and low by the mind that conceived them, comes at times to regard them as feeble shadows moving aimlessly about the light obscuring it" (*CW,* 74). Although he is dissatisfied with the myth as a total metaphysical explanation (after all, Plato leaves no room for the artist in his ideal City, as Stephen Dedalus points out in *Ulysses*),[20] Joyce tries to integrate it,

to rewrite it into the system he is evolving. In particular he sub-
stitutes for Plato's Idea the Hegelian concept of "Ideal,"[21]
which is the Idea realized in accordance with its concept. As
Bosanquet comments, "the Idea *qua* beautiful in art is not the
Idea as such, in the mode in which a metaphysical logic appre-
hends it as the absolute, but the Idea as developed into concrete form fit for reality, and as having entered into immediate
and adequate unity with this reality."[22] Thus understood as a
concrete reality synthesizing the Idea and its form, the Ideal will
be the proper object for the mind to elaborate and transform.
The elaboration, common to both romantics and classicists, is
curiously, ambiguously presented by Joyce with reference to
fire (shadows blown high and low), and sight ("a deeper insight" is a phrase that, as so often with Joyce, deserves to be
read literally as well as metaphorically; see also Ruskin's "pen-
etrative imagination"). This is a remarkable evocation and
connection, suggestive of the quasi-mystical quality of the epiphanic experience, which, because of its very ambiguity, he
wished to explore and clarify into theory. Let us also note his
exact use of words: "unrest"[23] is necessary, as it indicates the
essential duality of the Ideal, but "impatience" is to be de-
plored because it leads to the neglect and depreciation of the
sensible and betrays an inadequate relation to time. "Impatience" characterizes a type of mysticism that short-circuits
mind and method[24] and is to be contrasted with "applied mysticism." There again Joyce, though ostensibly passing judgment and setting up norms, is actually sounding the uneasy
workings of the artistic conscience, for, as he himself admits,
"the cause of the impatient temper must be sought in the artist
and in his theme" (*CW,* 75).

The other departure from the Neo-Hegelian line lies in a
presentation of the Idea in psychological terms, as "temper,"
especially in the conclusion to the first section, a rather long
introductory paragraph:

> Finally it must be asked concerning every artist how he is in re-
> lation to the highest knowledge and to those laws which do not
> take holiday because men and times forget them. This is not to

look for a message but to approach the temper which has made the work, an old woman praying, or a young man fastening his shoe, and to see what is there well done and how much it signifies. A song by Shakespeare or Verlaine, which seems so free and living and as remote from any conscious purpose as rain that falls in a garden or the lights of evening, is discovered to be the rhythmic speech of an emotion otherwise incommunicable, at least so fitly. But to approach the temper which has made art is an act of reverence and many conventions must be first put off, for certainly the inmost region will never yield to one who is enmeshed with profanities. (*CW,* 75)

This conclusion immediately follows Joyce's discussion of poetry and literature, and it clarifies his position in regard to the former and to language in general. The initial distinction he makes between the "message" and what "the work . . . signifies" is remarkable and is tantamount to the modern distinction between "signified" and "signifier." No less remarkable is the substantive importance given to the latter: the signifier, duly elaborated, makes sense, an *enigmatic* sense that calls for interpretative reading. In a song a *voice* is heard, expressive of "something" utterly remote from our conscious, self-contained life and causing another voice in us to manifest itself, just as our *gaze* can be held captive by the gaze that a picture seems to address us in an endless visual dialogue. A few pages later he will insistently present James Clarence Mangan as a composer of songs: "All his poetry remembers wrong and suffering and the aspiration of one who has suffered and who is moved to great cries and gestures when that sorrowful hour rushes upon the heart. This is the theme of a hundred songs but of none so intense as these songs which are made in noble misery, as his favorite Swedenborg would say, out of the vastation of soul" (*CW,* 80).

It may be felt that we are making Joyce unduly modern. Is he not? Such, after all, was his deliberate effort, in which he was only enlisting the help, and following the lead, offered by established thinkers, the better to clarify his own position. Indeed, his conciliation of the classical and the romantic schools was echoing Bosanquet's effort at establishing a continuity between ancient and modern theory: for the former, beauty is characterized by *rhythm*, symmetry, harmony of parts and whole, in short, unity in diversity; for the latter, beauty is inseparable from the notions of "*significance*, expressiveness, the *utterance* of all that life contains." The task of the modern theorist is to conciliate the abstract expressiveness of the former with the concrete expressiveness of the latter. Now, as early as the Greeks, *song* proves to be one of the first steps in the direction of such a synthesis. For Plato imitative or dramatic music is not acceptable in the commonwealth[25] because it is "concretely reproductive of natural reality, and therefore not expressive of ideas nor related to life in any way that he is able to comprehend." However, simple song tunes are acceptable to him (partly) "because they have an unrivalled capacity of symbolizing elementary moods and ideas."[26] Those rhythms or melodies are "'imitations' of certain types of life or *temper*."[27] In short, *"the limit between the image and the symbol is overstepped,"* and the reading of signs becomes the proper method of approach to artwork, plastic, pictorial, or poetic. The rapprochement of Shakespeare and Verlaine is significant, for both stand at turning points in the history of aesthetics: the former as the inaugurator of "the age of romantic classicism or modern classical naturalism,"[28] the latter as one of the standard bearers of modern symbolism.[29] Indeed, Joyce's distinction of literature and poetry on the very same page owes something to Verlaine's famous conclusion to "Art poétique," "Et tout le reste est littérature." But Joyce's handling of the concepts reveals his embarrassment: literature, the art of letters, is not dismissed outright as "ephemeral writing"; it is defined as an intermediate domain, halfway to poetry, which may welcome Wordsworth or Baudelaire, whose pieces are often encumbered with explicit message. However, a song (or a picture, for that matter) that is truly poetic is "discovered" to be so through a reading of signs. When Joyce copied down his paragraph into *Stephen Hero,* he prefaced it this way: "The critic is he who is able, by means of the *signs* which the artist affords, to approach . . . etc." (*SH,* 79). We would today describe these signs as signifiers, or possibly letters (depending on our critical allegiance): (1) they are not considered in terms of message and radically unrelated to any signified; and (2) they are not, as any sign would be, addressed to somebody.[30] As "rhythmic speech," they are made to play mutually in terms of pure contrasts, as signifiers should; (3) being "remote from any conscious purpose," they are not addressed to any one person, but to the Other: an Other explicitly presented as some Unconscious, and one also that carried a definite religious aura: to approach it is "an act of reverence . . . the inmost region will never yield to one who is enmeshed with profanities"; the atmosphere is definitely epiphanic, complete with a revolt against actuality and the "nets flung at [the soul] to hold it back from flight" (*PA*, 203).

Joyce is hovering along the border separating image and symbol, imagination and actual signifier, a region no doubt mapped out by his predecessors, Bosanquet's *A History of Aesthetic,* and other readings suggested by him (among others), but the exploration of which is motivated by, and conducted in, personal experience. The portrait of a brother poet, a canvas set in the frame of theory, was an opportunity for self-exploration through a highly complex, multidimensional portrait, which opens up like the petals of a flower (Dante's rose?) as we read. Mangan is depicted as a romantic, or neoromantic, "poète maudit,"[31] complete with exotic vices, unconventional attire, and the disdain, if not antagonism, of the Philistine, mainly those of the nationalistic persuasion.[32] Joyce keeps to his distinction between tradition and historical conditions: "Mangan, it must be remembered, wrote with no native literary tradition to guide him, and for a public which cared for matters of the day, and for poetry only so far as it might illustrate these" (*CW,* 78). But Mangan is presented as belonging to a well-established, honorable lineage, including Giacomo Leopardi, Novalis, Edgar Allan Poe, Robert Browning, Walter Pater, Walt Whitman, Paul Verlaine, Percy Bysshe Shelley, and William Blake, who are major references. Their presences are mainly felt through apparently incidental quotations.

Shelley appears briefly[33] in a quotation that, however, Joyce feels to be of such central import that he repeats and comments upon it in *A Portrait of the Artist:* "The best of what he has written makes its appeal surely, because it was conceived by the imagination, which he called, I think, the mother of things, whose dreams are we, who imageth us to herself, and to ourselves, and imageth herself in us—the power before whose breath the mind in creation is (to use Shelley's image) as a fading coal" (*CW,* 78). Here is Shelley's text, from his *Defence of Poetry:* "A man cannot say 'I will compose poetry.' The greatest poet even cannot say it; for the mind in creation is as a fading coal, which some invisible influence, like an inconstant wind, awakens to transitory brightness; this power arises from within, like the color of a flower which fades and changes as it developed, and the conscious portions of our natures are unprophetic either of its approach or of its departure."[34] And here is the context in which the image is set in *A Portrait of the Artist* (Joyce, through Stephen Dedalus, has been presenting anew his theory of the epiphany—though he carefully avoids the word—imported from *Stephen Hero,* and is now concluding):

> This supreme quality [the scholastic *quidditas,* Stephen suggests] is felt by the artist when the esthetic image is first conceived in his imagination. The mind in that mysterious instant Shelley likened beautifully to a fading coal. The instant wherein that supreme quality of beauty, the clear radiance of the esthetic image is apprehended luminously by the mind which has been arrested by its wholeness and fascinated by its harmony is the luminous silent stasis of esthetic pleasure, a spiritual state very like to that cardiac condition which the Italian physiologist Luigi Galvani, using a phrase almost as beautiful as Shelley's, called the enchantment of the heart. (*PA,* 213)

It is difficult at this point to decide whether Joyce fully assents to Mangan's theory of imagination. Joyce's commentary bears traces of an at least partial adherence to Neoplatonic doctrine, perhaps kindled by the public fervor of *fin-de-siècle* enthusiasts, including Yeats.[35] It also appears clearly personal in retrospect. And his theoretical formulations of the epiphany hinge on the Catholic doctrine concerning the Trinity and its rich Neoplatonic overtones. Above all, the image of the fading

coal insistently formulates something essential, and characteristically paradoxical, in Joyce's aesthetic experience: a fading of
the subject, a temporary *aphanisis* coincident with an exceptional moment of artistic activity. The evocation of this symbolic death is reinforced in *A Portrait of the Artist* with
Galvani's phrase, "the enchantment of the heart." As James
Atherton points out, "Galvani used the word *incantesimo,* enchantment, to describe the momentary cessation of the heart-
beat produced by inserting a needle into a frog's spinal cord."
The image now is no longer visual and imaginary, but metrical
and symbolic: the heart and its actual *rhythm,* suggestive of life
and death, of the suspension of life concomitant with the birth
of poetry.

Joyce's reference to a phenomenon borrowed from contemporary science is characteristic in another respect as well. He is
putting into practice his advocacy of vivisection, upon which
we have already remarked, betraying by the same token his per-
manent interest in experimental approaches. Was not, after all,
Mangan himself experimenting in more ways than one, in his
use of drugs for one thing, in his systematic recourse to excess
("in the end it is only his excesses that save him from indifference" *CW,* 77), and also in his forays into foreign cultures and
languages?

> The lore of many lands goes with him always, eastern tales and
> the memory of curiously printed medieval books which have
> rapt him out of his time—gathered together day by day and em-
> broidered as in a web. He has acquaintance with a score of lan-
> guages, of which, upon occasion, he makes a liberal parade, and
> has read recklessly in many literatures, crossing how many seas,
> and even penetrating into Peristan, to which no road leads that
> the feet travel. In Timbuctooese, he confesses with a charming
> modesty which should prevent detractors, he is slightly deficient,
> but this is no cause for regret. He is interested, too, in the life of
> the seeress of Prevorst, and in all phenomenon of the middle na-
> ture and here, where most of all the sweetness and resoluteness
> of the soul have power, he seems to seek in a world, how differ-
> ent from that in which Watteau may have sought, both with a
> certain graceful inconstancy, "what is there in no satisfying mea-
> sure or not at all." (*CW,* 77–78)

Typically again, excess, or the crossing of borders, the transgression of limits, is formulated in physical terms, as adventures of the *body*, mysterious, alluring, and dangerous at the
same time (remember that Timbuctoo, for long "the forbidden
city," had fallen into the hands of the French in 1894, only a
few years before Joyce was writing): adventures of the body
that were also adventures into the opacity of the signifier, the
crossing of the borders of the maternal tongue (whichever that
was), the desire to listen to the Other in foreign tongues and
to *reinject* it into the maternal tongue or text. Indeed, Joyce insists, "Is it not the deep sense of sorrow and bitterness which
explains these names [Naomi and Mara] and titles and this fury
of translation in which he has sought to lose himself?" (*CW*,
80). Names, those asemantic vocables, signifiers *par excellence*,
which we know, at least since Claude Lévi-Strauss's *The Elementary Structures of Kinship*, to be the cornerstones of symbolic structures, are indeed a matter of constant questioning,
nay, anguish, with James Clarence Mangan. "The Worst Loss"
is a poem about the loss of one's name, as is, in a sense, "The
Nameless One," Joyce's favorite piece; and "Naomi would
change her name to Mara, because it has gone bitterly with
her." Joyce betrayed the same anguish when he decided to sign
his private correspondence, not merely his public literary production, "Stephen Dedalus."

For Joyce, the fascination that Mangan held for him lay in
the enigma of his specific relation to "manque-à-être," or
"manque-à-naître" (I refrain from the more pointed, but also
more aggressive "Mangan-être"): the *enigmatic knot of excess
and loss*,[36] which, far from suggesting a life model, insistently
conveyed the existential anguish of a poet, the question of the
ethical choices in an aesthetic adventure: a confrontation with
the crux of the aesthetic paradox, "'obscure conception' *qua*
obscure, that is knowledge in the form of feeling and remaining
in that form."[37]

Joyce's only ground for dissent, if not disapproval, lay in the
wavering quality of Mangan's ethical stance. Joyce's twofold
criticism was bearing on what he felt was a very serious matter.
Mangan's flaw was such that he went adrift and foundered. His

writings failed to connect actively, and thus significantly, with his culture and to have any effect on it. It was of no moment, in both acceptations of the word: being purely nostalgic, it had no impact. He

> cries out, in his life and his mournful verses, against the injustice of despoilers, but never laments a deeper loss than the loss of plaids and ornaments. He inherits the latest and worst part of a legend upon which the line has never been drawn out and which divides against itself as it moves down the cycles. And because this tradition is so much with him he has accepted it with all its griefs and failures, and has not known how to change it, as the strong spirit knows, and so would bequeath it. (*CW,* 81–82)

Again, Joyce demonstrates the havoc caused by mental servitude, especially when it manifests itself under the seductive guise of nostalgic history, which conceals symbolic Loss of the Object with imaginary losses of object. Such a lack of distance, such an alienation, paralyses any symbolic activity (a redundant phrase, because an act, as *praxis,* is by nature symbolic). History is, or should be, not what you *imagine,* but what you *write:* its acceptable sense supposes freedom from images, bound to become clichés, and an *act of inscription* (literally and metaphorically), the choice of a writing subject who decides to establish, reestablish, displace the limit "between what can be 'comprehended' and what should be forgotten."[38] When Joyce says that Mangan "inherits the latest and worst part of a legend upon which the line has never been drawn out and which divides against itself as it moves down the cycles," every word counts. Mangan is a partial as well as passive inheritor who accepts submission to "what is to be read" (legend, the richly storied, edifying lives of great "saints") monotonously, a confused and repetitive farrago which has not be (re)ordered by the *act* of a subject assuming his own limit, his own symbolic castration, whose punctuation alone makes for intelligibility.

Typically, Joyce here does not use the Hogarthian phrase "the line of beauty," which he uses elsewhere,[39] because he wishes first and foremost to contrast this symbolic line with the notion of "division." The concept evokes Aristotelian method, an indispensable one in that it is the basic logical tool in the production of definitions;[40] it proved particularly useful in the definition of the soul.[41] In the present context, however, the biblical connotations and implications are far more relevant. Division against oneself is the very opposite of the symbolic order, in other words diabolic disorder (Matt. 12:25–26). Diabolic, perverse structure, as binary, manipulates the subject, robbing him of mediation, of the third term that enables him to relate to the Other through absence and the Word. The Devil works through *mirages* presenting good, desirable *images* worthy to be possessed and that ultimately make for ambivalent, diabolic possession; that is, the alienation and death of the subject.[42] Now Joyce feels Mangan has fallen slave to such images, which is the fatal flaw. "He is seen going forward alone like one who does penance for some ancient sin. Surely life, which Novalis has called a malady of the spirit, is a heavy penance for him who has, perhaps, forgotten the sin that laid it upon him" (*CW*, 76). In short, no *felix culpa* for him. For him sin exists in imaginary history only, not by reason of its symbolic roots (Original Sin, Christ's birth and death). The nature of memory, oblivion, and faith is perverted and turns hope and salvation into irrelevant questions, if not mockery. He has been beaten by the Devil's strategy, which has driven him through false hopes to ultimate damnation.

Joyce's portrait of Mangan encapsulates other portraits—not so much portraits of other poets, strangely enough, as portraits, or effigies, of women. And again, typically, diabolically should we say, we are presented with *one* portrait, that of Woman, seen from two contradictory angles. The first one occurs as an illustration of the workings and productions of Mangan's imagination: "Though even in the best of Mangan the presence of alien emotions is sometimes felt the presence of an imaginative personality reflecting the light of imaginative beauty is more vividly felt" (*CW*, 78). It is as much as saying that the vital center of his poetic activity is the production of self-portraits, however disguised in exotic garments: "East and West meet in that personality . . . ; images interweave there like soft luminous scarves and words ring like brilliant mail, and whether the song is of Ireland or of Istambol it has the same refrain, a prayer that peace may come again to her who has lost her peace, the moonwhite pearl of his soul, Ameen" (*CW,* 78). The text produced ("interweave") is gradually discovered, through male and female images, to be addressed to a woman's figure with whom reconciliation is sought, a reconciliation that sounds strikingly like the symbolic final enunciation in the Judeo-Christian tradition, "Amen," and so becomes the (impossible) Names of the Other. Joyce here is alluding to Mangan's poem "The Last Words of Al-Hassan." But he does not rest content with this evocation. He adds his own interminable last words:

> Music and odours and lights are spread about her, and he would search the dews and the sands that he might set another glory near her face. A scenery and a world have grown up about her face, as they will about any face which the eyes have regarded with love. Vittoria Colonna and Laura and Beatrice—even she upon whose face many lives have cast that shadowy delicacy, as of one who broods upon distant terrors and riotous dreams, and that strange stillness before which love is silent, Mona Lisa—embody one chivalrous idea, which is no mortal thing, bearing it bravely above the accidents of lust and faithlessness and weariness; and she whose white and holy hands have the virtue of enchanted hands, his virgin flower, and flower of flowers, is no less than these an embodiment of that idea. How the East is laid under tribute for her and must bring all its treasures to her feet! The sea that foams upon saffron sands, the lonely cedar on the Balkans, the hall damanscened with moons of gold and a breath of roses from the gulistan—all these shall be where she is in willing service: reverence and peace shall be the service of the heart, as in the verses "To Mihri":
>> My starlight, my moonlight, my midnight, my noonlight,
>> Unveil not, unveil not! (*CW,* 78–79)

Joyce consciously and explicitly offers a purple passage in direct imitation of Pater's famous word portrait of Mona Lisa in *Studies in the History of the Renaissance.* But, as is usual with Joyce, the allusion is not gratuitously decorative. He completes it with the evocation not only of a scenery, as in the background of a Renaissance portrait, but of a whole world, that of courtly love in which desire finds an ingenious solution to the insoluable problem of sexual relationship.[43] Following the lead of courtly poets, Joyce *writes* the solution, the impossible relation of man and woman into a poetic prose that is truly his own. The name chosen by Mangan for "the moonwhite pearl of his soul, Ameen," speaks for itself: it can be analyzed, with Skeat's help, into "'Amen,' from Hebrew *amen,* firm, true faithful, from verb *aman,* to sustain, support, found, fix, orig. 'to be firm.'"

What was it that Joyce, after Mangan, wished to "support, found, fix" with reference to the courtly ideal? An awful experience, though bearing the hallmark of necessity, one that was at the heart of his being, and too terrible to be faced in naked truth but only through the veil of beauty. In the concluding lines from "To Mihri," the beauty of the starry dome is ambiguously epiphanic, a revelation from another world conveyed in terms, and from the standpoint, of this our sublunary world. For here, as in "To Amine, on seeing her about to veil her mirror," the suggestion is that of a dangerous and forbidden territory, that of death, that is, the moment when mirrors should be veiled.

Toward the close of his lecture, Joyce goes a step further in the portrait inspired to him by Mangan's poetry:

> In the final view the figure which he worships is seen to be an abject queen upon whom, because of the bloody crimes that she has done and of those as bloody that were done to her, madness is come and death is coming, but who will not believe that she is near to die and remembers only the rumor of voices challenging her secret gardens and her fair, tall flowers that have become the food of boars. Novalis said of love that it is the Amen of the universe, and Mangan can tell of the beauty of hate; and pure hate is as excellent as pure love. (*CW,* 82)

Joyce's dramatic portrait offers a resolution of the plot somehow implicit in "Ibsen's New Drama." Abjection is now revealed as a ruling power, in its essential connection with the symbolic function. It is identified as sadistic crime, as the process through which "man finds a way of cooperating in new creations of nature. The central idea is that nature's impetus is hampered by its own forms, that the three kingdoms, by producing fixed forms, imprison nature into a cramped cycle."[44] Crime is a possible producer of new and beautiful forms: Mangan can tell of "the beauty of hate," which is merely the reverse side of love. Such creative, poetic activity is truly symbolic in that it creates new laws, new cycles, new *names*: "The ancient gods, who are visions of the divine names, die and come to life many times, though there is dusk about their feet and darkness in their indifferent eyes, the miracle of light is renewed eternally in the imaginative soul" (*CW,* 83).

Hence the ambiguous attitude to death and the death drive, present in most of Mangan's writings. Mangan's poems had been "made in noble misery, as his favorite Swedenborg would say, out of the vastation of soul" (*CW,* 80). Swedenborg's phrase describes a purifying ordeal. But what Joyce divines, or at least lays bare, in the writings of Mangan is what it is that he tries to purify himself of, and the way in which he tries to exorcise the awful hold of disease and death, of sheer horror, over him. Joyce points out how this horror is both veiled and made present through the image, the portrait of a woman assumed to be Woman, and through her name, well meant to sound to our ears like the final utterance and punctuation of any address to the Other.

Although fascinated by this kindred soul, Joyce ultimately distances himself from Mangan, "this feeble-bodied figure" that he believes has fallen a victim of "a narrow and hysterical nationality." The recurring word of Joyce's last two paragraphs, through a variety of allusions to Ibsen, Hauptmann, and Theosophy, is "life," joyful life. Joyce reacts very much like Nietzsche, whose praise of life is a positive nonreactive attitude to disease:

> When the sterile and treacherous order is broken up, a voice or a host of voices is heard singing, a little faintly at first, of a serene spirit which enters woods and cities and the hearts of men, and of the life of earth—det dejlige vidunderlige jordliv det gaadefulde jordliv—beautiful, alluring, mysterious.
>
> Beauty, the splendour of truth, is a gracious presence when

the imagination contemplates intensely the truth of its own being or the visible world, and the spirit which proceeds out of truth and beauty is the holy spirit of joy. These are realities and these alone give and sustain life. As often as human fear and cruelty, that wicked monster begotten by luxury, are in league to make life ignoble and sullen and to speak evil of death the time is come when a man of timid courage seizes the keys of hell and of death, and flings them far out into the abyss, proclaiming the praise of life, which the abiding splendour of truth may sanctify, and of death, the most beautiful form of life. In those vast courses which enfold us and in that great memory which is greater and more generous than our memory, no life, no moment of exaltation is ever lost; and all those who have written nobly have not written in vain, though the desperate and weary have never heard the silver laughter of wisdom. Nay, shall not such as these have part, because of that high, original purpose which remembering painfully or by way of prophecy they would make clear, in the continual affirmation of the spirit? (*CW,* 83)

Joyce endeavors to explore beyond conventional analysis of beauty and imagination, as well as beyond fashionable doctrines, which are only additional grist to his mill. Quite logically, his praise of life follows two main lines, focuses on two concepts: nature and symbolic enunciation.

Joyce's praise of the earth has of course nothing to do with, is exactly the opposite of, current Irish "peasant" ideology, for which he had nothing but disdain.[45] It is rather "that ardent sympathy with nature as it is—*natura naturata*" that he discovered, to his delight, in Giordano Bruno's philosophy, and that brought him into sympathy with Spinoza's.[46] A logical consequence of Joyce's insistence on the concrete as integral to symbolic activity is his shifting of focus toward the personality of the artist. Commenting upon artistic intelligence at the beginning of the lecture, he had inserted that "*so long as this place in nature is given us,* it is right that art should do no violence to that gift, though it may go far beyond the stars and the waters in the service of what it loves" (*CW,* 74, italics mine), thus paraphrasing to his own better purpose Hegel's analysis of consciousness in its relation to creation and art: "Man breaks the boundary of merely potential and immediate consciousness, so that just for the reason that he knows himself to be an animal, he ceases to be an animal and, as *mind,* attains to self-knowledge."[47] The initial reservation in Joyce's statement ("so long as this place," etc.) is not empty rhetoric. It reveals his awareness of human frailty, of how human nature is ever tottering on the brink of animality and barbarism and madness, an awareness born of the very images that narcissistically fascinated him, a legendary queen (Queen Maeve?), a traditional figure in the history of Irish poetry, or (why not?) a phantasmic avatar of the Virgin Mary.

As his first portrait of the artist, "James Clarence Mangan" goes a step further than "Ibsen's New Drama" as a structural analysis of desire, *jouissance,* and (sexual) relationship. It presents a study in self-expression as an enigma: what ultimately is the meaning of Mangan's "excesses that save him from indifference"? What is his strange dress "a half-conscious expression" of? What part is he suspected to have played "in a love-comedy of three" (*CW,* 77)? and so forth. The romantic theme of unrest ("the condition of all achievement"), combined with morbid ethical weakness, has become a problem: "Because this [Irish] tradition is so much with him he has accepted it with all its griefs and failures, and has not known how to change it, as the strong spirit knows, and so would bequeath it: the poet who hurls his anger against tyrants would establish upon the future an intimate and far more cruel tyranny" (*CW,* 82). The problem remains the ethical one of servitude versus will, of the answer of the "soul" to "reality," and, inextricably, an aesthetic one. What does the *body know,* obscurely but surely, of (human) *nature's laws,* and how does this knowledge connect with "those laws which do not take holiday because men and times forget them"? In a sense, Joyce reverses the usual pattern that appealed to so many of his contemporaries, for instance the "misty mystics," for whom knowledge was of the soul and movement of the body. Rather, he questions the knowledge of the body as expressive of significant movements of the soul. Biographical evidence at this stage is not out of place. That he was then preoccupied with the body had certainly something to do with the prurient puritanism of ambient Irish Catholicism. But the personal dimension was certainly decisive, especially his brother George's illness, which was to terminate in death a month later; several epiphanies testify to his sorrow and anguish.[48] In the last analysis, the intensity of these reactions points to basic structural attitudes, illustrated variously and insistently by his desire to become an actor, and above all by his desire to enter the medical profession: he registered with the Cecilia Street School of Medicine, Dublin, the following spring, before trying the Sorbonne in Paris at the end of the year (failing to gain admission only due to administrative reasons). "James Clarence Mangan" enables us to see beyond surface and anecdote into the heart of the matter. Indeed, from that moment on, we will observe him investigating the concept of nature, in its widest acceptation, as related to pantheism on the one hand, and to science, especially so-called psychology, the science of the soul, on the other. He was guided along the first path by Bosanquet's presentation of the Western tradition, notably Plotinus's contribution to aesthetic reflection, by Giordano Bruno's and Spinoza's pantheism. He has insisted on a philosophical approach of poetry and its problems, "poetry, with which is philosophy" (*CW*, 75), that Aristotle's *Poetics* could initiate, as it also could connect art and aesthetic to "scientific" analysis, the study of nature and the art of poetry. Or so he fondly hoped.

Philosophical investigation was not all, however. "James Clarence Mangan" was a portrait of a poet, not of The Poet. Its function for Joyce was to examine, against a background of history and tradition, the poetic *ethos,* not as perfect model, as he will seem to do later with William Blake (and in a different key with Daniel Defoe), but in its most ambivalent constitution, as capable of achievement, and also definitely this side of perfection, as related to the most secret, shameful flaws in human nature: at the moment when intellect, the mind is on the verge of total collapse, of losing its grasp of reality. A mediator liable to become a traitor, a poet may be most active when dissolving as presence and truth and identifying into his medium. Hence the aptness of Joyce's eucharistic metaphor for the poetic process, or *praxis,* which formulates the change in the status of both process and object: from imitative reproduction and images to symbolic enunciation and the play of signifiers and letters. The first attitude is negative and spells alienation: images, idols, connote passivity, indifference, fascination, and death. The second attitude, which begins by questioning the actual nature of imagination, will prove to approximate closely life and joy because it implies freedom from representation, and is an *act* in the fullest acceptation of the word, a symbolic transformation, as in the play of signifiers within a language or between several languages. Such are some of the problems that Joyce will eventually choose to study with the help, among others, of Aristotle and Aquinas.

"James Clarence Mangan" is a new stage in Joyce's delineation of his self-portrait. Strangely enough, one of its salient features is the theoretical frame into which it is set. Or not strangely, for it is a splendid frame, giving the right depth of perspective to his endeavor. Stylistically beautiful, it culminates in an explicit, though contextually ambiguous praise of beauty: the beauty of theory, *theoria,* contemplation, an antidote to what is presented *en abîme* (i.e., according to heraldry, both in a central position and totally unrelated to any other pattern or *piece*), the horror of woman's desire and mastery, leading to abjection and madness, when *jouissance* of the Other is at its most threatening. The Beauty of theory, Beauty contemplated in, through theory, in philosophical formulation. Beauty as *Amen,* as "fixion," to use Lacan's coinage, as a way (moment? method?) of fixing, of giving firmness to a soul ever tottering on the brink of abysses: totally distinct from the portrait of the subject, a discrete frame acting as bordering and *garde-fou.* Amen, the final word, as the invented figure of the original Name as Woman, La Femme.

CHAPTER FIVE

The Paris Notebook

·

THE PARIS NOTEBOOK, as edited in the *Critical Writings,* consists of six fragments of unequal length, each of them dated. The first and longest (longer than the remaining five put together) is dated 13 February 1903. It begins with definitions of desire and loathing and of "improper" art, then turns to a discussion of tragedy and comedy, before concluding on art in general. Now Joyce here, as in the case of the following fragments (on lyric, epic, and dramatic arts and on rhythm), starts from Bosanquet's criticism of Plato in chapter 4 of his *A History of Aesthetic,* "Signs of Progress in Greek Theory concerning the Beautiful." According to Bosanquet, Plato's position toward "the aesthetic principle" should be examined with reference to "the antithesis of abstract and concrete analysis," the question being "whether the pleasure is expected to arise from the sheer expressive effect of the aesthetic appearance, or from purposes or associations connected with the existence of the real objects of which that appearance reminds us" (Bosanquet, 50). It follows that the decisive distinction is not between "hedonistic" and "moralistic" arts, but "within the region of pleasurable presentation . . . in the contrast between pure and impure modes and conditions of such presentation."

Such is the distinction Joyce starts from in his first fragment: "Desire is the feeling which urges us to go to something, and loathing is the feeling which urges us to go from something;

and that art is improper which aims at exciting these feelings in us whether by comedy or by tragedy." As early as chapter 1, and quite logically in view of the philosophical import of aesthetic investigation, Bosanquet had presented "an approximate psychological definition of aesthetic enjoyment, 'Pleasure in the nature of a feeling or presentation, as distinct from pleasure in its momentary or expected stimulation of the organism.' Such pleasure [he added] would always, it is my belief, be connected in fact with the significance of the content, but the meeting-point of the psychological and metaphysical definitions would not fall within the scope of psychology" (Bosanquet, 7–8). And he could now invoke Aristotle: In *Probl.* 896b, "sexual preference is . . . contrasted with aesthetic selection, real beauty is distinguished from beauty which only has reference to desire" (Bosanquet, 62).

No wonder then if Joyce adopts such an approach and tries to advance beyond mere psychology:

> Tragedy aims at exciting in us feelings of pity and terror. Now terror is the feeling which arrests us before whatever is grave in human fortunes and unites us with its secret cause and pity is the feeling which arrests us before whatever is grave in human fortunes and unites us with the human sufferer. Now loathing, which in an improper art aims at exciting in the way of tragedy, differs, it will be seen, from the feelings which are proper to tragic art, namely terror and pity. For loathing urges us from rest because it urges us to go from something, but terror and pity hold us in rest, as it were, by fascination. When tragic art makes my body to shrink terror is not my feeling because I am urged from rest, and moreover this art does not show me what is grave, I mean what is constant and irremediable, in human fortunes nor does it unite me with any secret cause for it shows me only what is unusual and remediable and it unites me with a cause only too manifest. Nor is an art properly tragic which would move me to prevent human suffering any more than an art is properly tragic which would move me in anger against some manifest cause of human suffering. Terror and pity, finally, are aspects of sorrow comprehended in sorrow—the feeling which the privation of some good excites in us. (*CW*, 143–44)

In *A Portrait of the Artist,* shortly before repeating these definitions almost verbatim, Stephen Dedalus says, "Aristotle has not defined pity and terror" (204). He is wrong or insincere, because he could have found those definitions in the *Rhetoric* (II.5 and 8) if not in the *Poetics.* In any case, Bernays's famous commentary echoed by Butcher (chap. 6, "The Function of Tragedy"), as well as Bosanquet (65 and 235ff.), provided the basic argument: the medical sense of *katharsis,* purgation (upon which, incidentally, Joyce was soon to play all along his verse satire "The Holy Office"). Butcher, faithful to his general interpretation of the *Poetics,* comments on the theory: in tragedy, pity and terror are purged of the impure elements that associate with them in real life. It is true that Aristotle did not say so much, but it is perfectly legitimate to consider and complete his theory in the light of his philosophy. And this is exactly what Joyce undertakes here, using concepts borrowed from the *De anima* and the *Metaphysics:* the pattern of "causes," "Necessity" ("what is constant and irremediable in human fortunes"), and "sorrow comprehended in sorrow" ("actual" sensation is identical to its object).

Remarkably enough, Joyce's starting point is psychological even to the point of being almost personal. He seems intent on clarifying, or at least formulating, an experience that is very much his own, an experience in which he is paralyzed by some sort of hysterical effect ("arrests," "rest," "fascination"), which indeed unites him with both the suffering subject and the One as Cause. The experience, in short, is gradually revealed to be *metaphysical* in its implication: "what is grave in human fortunes," in *tuchès,* or encounters, is ultimately discovered to be "the privation of some good," as exile from the Good as the Secret Cause of Creation and of the individual creature.

Joyce here, rather than a commentator of Aristotle, is using the latter's philosophy to his own best purposes, with a view to formulating and distilling his own quasi-religious experience of the Real—a distillation that reveals, beyond desire itself, the dark core of deathly *jouissance,* another dimension of which he now proceeds to explore:

And now of comedy. An improper art aims at exciting in the way of comedy the feeling of desire but the feeling which is proper to comic art is the feeling of joy. Desire, as I have said, is the feeling which urges us to go to something but joy is the feeling which the possession of some good excites in us. Desire, the feeling which an improper art seeks to excite in the way of comedy, differs, it will be seen, from joy. For desire urges us from rest that we may possess something but joy holds us in rest so long as we possess something. Desire, therefore, can only be excited in us by a comedy (a work of comic art) which is not sufficient in itself inasmuch as it urges us to seek something beyond itself; but a comedy (a work of comic art) which does not urge us to seek anything beyond itself excites in us the feeling of joy. All art which excites in us the feeling of joy is so far comic and according as this feeling of joy is excited by whatever is substantial or accidental in human fortunes the art is to be judged more or less excellent: and even tragic art may be said to participate in the nature of comic art so far as the possession of a work of tragic art (a tragedy) excites in us the feeling of joy. From this it may be seen that tragedy is the imperfect manner and comedy the perfect manner in art. All art, again, is static for the feelings of terror and pity on the one hand and of joy on the other hand are feelings which arrest us. It will be seen afterwards how this rest is necessary for the apprehension of the beautiful—the end of all art, tragic or comic—for this rest is the only condition under which the images, which are to excite in us terror or pity or joy, can be properly presented to us and properly seen by us. For beauty is a quality of something seen but terror and pity and joy are states of mind. James A. Joyce, 13 Feb., 1903. (*CW*, 144–45)

In his efforts to lay the foundations of an aesthetic by developing some implications of the *Poetics*, Joyce extends the concept of comedy to cover any "work of comic art," which apparently raises more questions than it solves, for instance, those connected with the varieties of verbal comic, especially in view of his own later productions, from *Dubliners* through *Ulysses* to *Finnegans Wake*.

Extrapolations would be too easy here. However, what is worth pointing out is that by putting comedy above tragedy Joyce is simply following once more the suggestions of his

Neo-Hegelian masters—for instance, Butcher when he insists that "humour is the meeting-point of tragedy and comedy" (386) and, still more strikingly, Bosanquet, who spells out the full metaphysical implications of the comic: "Only that is truly comic, in which the persons of the play are comic for themselves as well as for the spectator, and so escape all seriousness, bitterness or disappointment when their futile purposes are destroyed by the means they take to realize them. Comedy starts from the *absolute reconciliation* which is the close of tragedy, the *absolute self-certainty and cheerfulness* which nothing can disturb" (Bosanquet, 360–361, italics mine). Bosanquet concludes with a long quotation from the close of Hegel's *Aesthetics:*

> With the development of comedy we have arrived at the close of our scientific discussion. . . . In this culmination comedy is leading straight to the *dissolution of art in general.* The aim of all art is the identity, produced by the mind, in which the eternal and divine, the substantively true, is revealed in *real appearance* and shape to our external perception, our feelings and our imagination. But if comedy displays this *unity only in its self-dissolution,* inasmuch as the Absolute, endeavouring to produce itself into reality, sees this realization destroyed by interests which have obtained freedom in the real world, and are directed only to the subjective and accidental, then the presence and activity of the Absolute no longer appears in positive union with the character and aims of real existence, but exclusively asserts itself in the negative form, that it destroys everything which does not correspond to it; and *only subjectivity as such displays itself* in this dissolution as self-confident and self-secure. (*CW,* 360–61, italics mine)

The analysis of tragic and comic arts by Joyce is another aspect of his exploration of the mechanisms of subjectivity, of the paradoxes of the subject in its relation to the Real and to the Other. On the one hand, the subject is plainly affected—and, so to speak, divided—in his or her experience of various "states of mind" that are at the heart of the aesthetic experience, and that modern psychology, Bosanquet insists again and again (see in particular 466–67), should examine more closely. On the other hand, "joy," as "the possession of some good" (note the symmetry with "the privation of some good" in tragedy) is *jouissance* as supreme, as possession of and by Love, as the ultimate rest and reconciliation with the Other. This is a stance that will quite logically lead Joyce to the theological questions of Love between the persons of the Holy Trinity in their mutual contemplation, of (beatific) vision and of the nature of images. And in a broader perspective, the encounter of beauty in, through images seen is only one aspect, one approach or formulation of a more general problem, that of the (symbolic) division of the modern subject (Bosanquet, 89, 93, 168–69) traceable to the Augustinian *cogito* (Bosanquet, 134, 172).

No wonder, then, that the subject, of necessity thus holding a central position, is also at the heart of the next fragment of Joyce's, dated 6 March 1903, which focuses on "mediation": "There are three conditions of art: the lyrical, the epical and the dramatic. That art is lyrical whereby the artist sets forth the image in immediate relation to himself; that art is epical whereby the artist sets forth the image in mediate relation to himself and to others; that art is dramatic whereby the artist sets forth the image in immediate relation to others. James A. Joyce, 6 March, 1903, Paris" (*CW*, 145).

We could have (in relation to "Drama and Life") discussed those three "conditions" as forming a pattern more or less analogous to Hegel's, Ruskin's, or the *Encyclopedia Britannica*'s. It is my contention that Joyce's actual inspiration was Butcher, according to whom "the Greek drama is the harmonious fusion of two elements which never before had been perfectly blended. Lyrical in its origin, epic in the nature of its materials, it is at once an expression of passionate feeling and the story of an action. It *embodies emotion,* but an emotion which *grows into will* and *issues in deeds*" (Butcher, 339–40). Butcher simply spells out the implications of his analysis of *mimesis,* whose three objects are *pathos, ethos,* and *praxis*—or, in his reformulation, the immediate lyrical experience born from *pathos,* the epical mediation as staging an *ethos,* and dramatic *praxis* as the truly symbolic act as of the subject.

But enough of sources. We would lose an essential aspect of

Joyce's research if we failed to emphasize the problem his dialectical argument aims at solving: the opposition, not to say
contradiction, between image and articulate speech, or Word,
or, to use Lacanian categories broadly, the Imaginary and the
Symbolic. Once more the question is how one can relate to the
Other (meaning the Word) through "others" without losing
oneself into the *One* of imaginary, narcissistic satisfaction.

It so appears that Joyce, following Butcher's and Bosanquet's
suggestions once more, looked for an answer in the concept of
rhythm, which he undertook to define and put to the best use
he could in his next two fragments:

> Rhythm seems to be the first or formal relation of part to part
> in any whole or of a whole to its part or parts, or of any part to
> the whole of which it is a part. . . . Parts constitute a whole as
> far as they have a common end.
>
> James A. Joyce, 25 March, 1903, Paris.

> *e tekhne mimeitai ten physin*—This phrase is falsely rendered as
> "Art is an imitation of Nature." Aristotle does not here define
> art; he says only, "Art imitates Nature" and means that the artis-
> tic process is like the natural process. . . . It is false to say that
> sculpture, for instance, is an art of repose if by that be meant that
> sculpture is unassociated with movement. Sculpture is associated
> with movement in as much as it is rhythmic; for a work of sculp-
> tural art must be surveyed according to its rhythm and this sur-
> veying is an imaginary movement in space. It is not false to say
> that sculpture is an art of repose in that a work of sculptural art
> cannot be presented as itself moving in space and remain a work
> of sculptural art.
>
> James A. Joyce, 27 March, 1903, Paris (*CW,* 145)

Joyce's interpretation of the famous Aristotelian tag, which
characteristically emphasizes the verb at the expense of the
noun, follows the presentation of Butcher in his chapter 1,
"Art and Nature" (see especially 116). Its value and function
were to lay the basis for, and give substance to, his definition
of rhythm and to the role he assigns to it. A missing link in the
argument can be discovered in the next chapter, "Imitation as
an Aesthetic Term," in which Butcher documents at length the
thesis that "music was held by Aristotle, as by the Greeks gen-

erally, to be the most 'imitative' or representative of the arts. It is a direct image, a copy of character" (Butcher, 128–29). Butcher quotes the *Politics* to support his argument ("In rhythms and melodies we have the most realistic imitations of anger and mildness as well as of courage, temperance and all their opposites," *Pol.* V.viii.5.1340a18), "the theoretic basis [being] that the external movements of rhythmical sound bear a close resemblance to the movements of the soul," as is illustrated in *Probl.* XIX.29.920a3 (Butcher, 132).

Beyond those immediate sources of Joyce's, a larger perspective opens in two directions. One is the historical interpretation and illustration of the thesis; the other is the more tentative line Joyce was following, or that, at least, we believe we are entitled to reconstruct. The first one is clearly indicated as early as Bosanquet's chapter 1: "Among the Ancients the fundamental theory of the beautiful was connected with the notions of rhythm, symmetry, harmony of parts; in short with the general formula of unity in variety" (Bosanquet, 4), and repeated and more fully spelt out in chapter 3, "The Fundamental Outlines of Greek Theory concerning the Beautiful": "The one true aesthetic principle recognized by Hellenic antiquity . . . may be described as the principle that beauty consists in the imaginative or sensuous expression of unity in variety" (30). Bosanquet does not hesitate to broaden the philosophical scene: "The synthesis of the one and the many was, as we all know, the central problem and the central achievement of Greek philosophy. The conception of unity in variety [Bosanquet soon adds the alternative formulation "the relation of whole to part," which Joyce echoes] is the indispensable basis of that idea of *system* or totality of independent parts, which was destined to be *the structure erected by modern speculation upon the definite* foundation laid by the Greek thinkers" (32, italics mine; see also 33 for the quotation from *Met.* 1078a).

Joyce's definition now assumes its full significance. It aims at giving the formal principle a philosophical formulation by borrowing Aristotle's own categories, and that is why he was at pains to master not only the *Poetics* but also the Aristotelian system (see Appendix B). As in his definition of terror and pity, though less explicitly, his reference is to the concept of *cause;* in both cases, the aim is to provide for art as an imitation, in the sense defined above, of *nature,* a rationale based on the same concept. The problem was becoming an epistemological one; if true science is the science of causes, the "science of aesthetic" is bound to be the "science of aesthetic causes," in their relation to natural causes.

Now again rhythm is tentatively defined in terms of "formal" and "final" ("end") causes. Joyce deliberately shuns any physical simile suggesting organic development. The type of relation his definition describes is neither linear nor chronological, but structural, quite in the spirit of the definition of tragedy given in *Poetics* (VII.i.4 and VIII.4).

In short, after examining relations in terms of the external conditions of art, Joyce is now considering them "from inside." As Stephen Dedalus said to Lynch with reference to his aesthetic theory, "we are just now in a mental world" (*PA*, 206). Butcher had made it quite clear to Joyce:

> A work of poetic art, as [Aristotle] conceives it, while it manifests the universal is yet a concrete and individual reality, a coherent whole, animated by a living principle—or by something which is at least the counterpart of life—and framed according to the laws of organic beauty. The artistic product is not indeed in a literal sense alive; for life or soul is in Aristotle the result of the proper form being impressed upon the proper matter. Now in art the matter depends on the choice of the artist; it has no *necessary* relation to the form which is impressed on it. That form it passively receives, but it is not thereby endowed with any active principle of life or movement. The form or essence lives truly only in the mind of the artist who conceived the work, and it is *in thought alone* that it is transferred to the dead matter with which it has no natural affinity. The *artist, or the spectator* who has entered into the artist's thought, by a *mental act* lends life to the artistic creation; he speaks, he thinks of it as a thing of life; but it has no inherent principle of movement; it is in truth not alive but merely the semblance of a living reality. (Butcher, 189–90, italics mine)

Joyce's notes on "intelligence," "speculation," and "thought" (see Appendix B) are to be read as an effort at effecting a conciliation of Aristotelian *nous* and modern conceptions of mental activity.

In order to support his statement, Butcher quotes not only the *De Partibus Animalium* and the *De Generatione Animalium*, but even more pointedly Stewart's edition of the *Nichomachean Ethics:* "*Tekhne* realizes its good in an extended *ergon*, and the *eidos* which it imposes on *hylé* is only a surface form—very different from the forms penetrating to the very heart of the *hylé*, which *physis* and *areté* produce" (*Nic. Ethics* II.42). This quotation again illuminates Joyce's note from the *Metaphysics:* "The wood does not make the bed nor the bronze the statue" (see Appendix B).

Now it must be observed that Joyce's definition of rhythm in terms purely of formal and final causes implicitly points out that what difficulties remain concern the material and the efficient causes; this coincides with Butcher's commentary posing the problem of the choice of the "proper" matter depending on the choice of the artist. The problem is that of new logical matter, and a new type of necessity. In his definition of rhythm Joyce plays with notions of "parts" and "end" in a manner that introduces another dimension into the pattern, a sort of retrospective dimension: he emphasizes a concept of differed, or after-, *effect* insofar as significance is then constructed from the end backward. Parts are what you start from, but their rhythm as significance is revealed only in their final coincidence.

Let us go a step further in this unfolding of Joyce's notes, this deciphering of his theoretical shorthand. Part-ition comes to the fore as the touchstone of his aesthetic discourse, insofar as it creates a *logical* (*Logos*, discourse) structure, not a linear, or chronological, sequence. And rhythm may be considered as his first, provisional answer, in terms of theory, to a question certainly relevant to poetic practice at large. There is a clear indication of its nature when he established the lyrical basis of all discursive production. Numerous passages from his works may be adduced at this point as illustrations of his actual purpose. One of the best known is in *A Portrait of the Artist:* "The lyrical form is in fact the simplest verbal vesture of an instant of emotion, a rhythmical cry such as ages ago cheered on the man who pulled at the oar or dragged stones up a slope" (*PA*, 214). And again on the next page: "The personality of the artist, at first a cry or a cadence or a mood" (*PA*, 215). *Ulysses* also bears traces of this early theorizing, for example at the beginning of "Proteus," with the passage beginning with "Rhythm begins you see" (*U*, 37), or in "Circe" (*U*, 432–33).

So *rhythm,* or *gesture* for that matter, as expressive, as the meeting point of man's inner and outer worlds, assumes a metaphysical significance, suggestive of a world "beyond nature." Akin to entelechy (see Appendix B), it gives access to Being. The paradox, though, is that this act is one of partitioning. At this stage in his analysis of expressive relations, Joyce uses rhythm, or rather the concept of rhythm, in order to establish this act as basic to the logic, the *discursive* and *symbolic* dimension of aesthetic production. It is revealed as a speech act creating the symbolic break, or gap (or, as Lacan would have said, castration), which is the precondition, the necessary moment preliminary to significant presentation.

In this context, the break initiated by a certain type of cry (would it not be the case to speak of a "primal cry"?) indicated access into the order of pure (poetic) *signifiers,* this side of conventional meanings as conveyed by "words": *cry* and *word* are the two sides of the linguistic coin. It has been observed that in *A Portrait of the Artist* Stephen Dedalus's progress in symbolic self-expression is punctuated, at the end of each chapter, by a cry: this is only a more sophisticated version of the experiments conducted by the same character in *Stephen Hero* when he endeavors to "construct cries for primitive emotions" (32).

Poetic construction, indeed, is what engaged Joyce's interest in the next, and last, series of notes in the Paris Notebook:

> Art is the human disposition of sensible or intelligible matter for an aesthetic end.
> James A. Joyce, 28 March, 1903, Paris.

> Question: Why are not excrements, children, and lice works of art?
> Answer: Excrements, children, and lice are human products—

93

human dispositions of sensible matter. The process by which they are produced is natural and non-artistic; their end is not an aesthetic end: therefore, they are not works of art.

Question: Can a photograph be a work of art?

Answer: A photograph is a disposition of sensible matter and may be so disposed for an aesthetic end but it is not a human disposition of sensible matter. Therefore it is not a work of art.

Question: If a man hacking in fury at a block of wood make there an image of a cow (say) has he made a work of art?

Answer: The image of a cow made by a man hacking in fury at a block of wood is a human disposition of sensible matter but it is not a human disposition of sensible matter for an aesthetic end. Therefore it is not a work of art.

Question: Are houses, clothes, furniture, etc., works of art?

Answer: Houses, clothes, furniture, etc., are not necessarily works of art. They are human dispositions of sensible matter. When they are so disposed for an aesthetic end they are works of art. (*CW*, 145–46)

In *A Portrait of the Artist*, Stephen Dedalus says:

> I have a book at home . . . in which I have written down questions. . . . In finding the answers to them I found the theory of aesthetic which I am trying to explain. Here are some questions I set myself: *"Is a chair finely made tragic or comic? Is the portrait of Mona Lisa good if I desire to see it? Is the bust of Sir Philip Crampton lyrical, epical or dramatic? Can excrements or a child or a louse be a work of art? If not, why not?"* (214; see also *SH*, 77)

As we now know, the list was longer than that (see also Appendix B), and Joyce's intellectual process was clearly different from Stephen's, which seems to have followed more or less the pattern of Aristotle's *Problemata*, whereas here questions and answers are apparently presented catechistically as practical applications of an axiomatic definition. Rather than the full-grown, full-blown artistic genius that Stephen is supposed to be, Joyce is a theorist busily establishing the epistemological basis of aesthetic science.

"Sensible or intelligible matter" refers to the aspects of any aesthetic system: the conciliation of a theory of the sensible with a theory of Beauty. The latter will be examined in the Pola

Notebook in terms of the Aquinian intellectual system. No wonder then if, at this point, Joyce's catechism confines itself to a verification of his axiom as regards "sensible matter," obviously reserving the problems connected with "intelligible matter" for future examination. Joyce appears quite coherently to follow here again the logic and the categories of the Aristotelian system, this time through an implicit reference to the *Nichomachean Ethics,* which sheds a good deal of light on his perspective, not so much book 1, which indeed forms, at least in part, the background of the Pola Notebook, as indeed book 6, chapters 3 and 4. Chapter 3, after listing the "five truth attaining virtues"—namely, Art, Scientific Knowledge, Prudence, Wisdom, and Intelligence—treats "Scientific Knowledge" in the following terms:

> We all conceive that a thing which we know scientifically cannot vary; when a thing that can vary is beyond the range of our observation, we do not know whether it exists or not. An object of Scientific Knowledge, therefore, exists of necessity. . . . Scientific Knowledge . . . is the quality whereby we demonstrate, with the further qualifications included in our definition of it in the *Analytics* [*An. Post.* I.71b9ff.], namely, that a man knows a thing scientifically when he possess a conviction arrived at in a certain way, and when the first principles on which that conviction rests are known to him with certainty—for unless he is more certain of his first principles than of the conclusion drawn from them he will only possess the knowledge in question *accidentally.* (*Nicomachean Ethics,* Loeb Classical Library, 331–35, italics mine)

Joyce's axiomatic definition of art aims at giving artistic activity and artistic productions a scientific standing (the pending question being the "aesthetic end"; i.e., the experience of the Beautiful), to be confirmed and developed in the four corollaries that follow.

If we move from method to the actual contents of the definition and of the questions and answers, we must turn to chapter 4, where Aristotle examines art and concludes:

> An Art is the same thing as a rational quality, concerned with making [i.e., radically distinct from doing] that reasons truly. All

Art deals with bringing something into existence; and to pursue an art means to study how to bring into existence a thing which may either exist or not, and the efficient cause of which lies in the maker and not in the thing made; for Art does not deal with things that exist or come into existence of necessity, or according to nature, since these have their efficient cause in themselves. . . . In a sense *Art deals with the same objects as Chance,* as Agathon says: Chance is beloved of Art, and Art of Chance. (*Nicomachean Ethics,* Loeb Classical Library, 335)

One central question remains for Joyce to answer: how can one solve the contradiction between Chance, *tuchè,* and scientific perspective? That is why Joyce's catechism, though it sounds as a mere mechanical application of his, and Aristotle's definition, is really more complex and problematic than may appear at first. The first answer is indeed purely mechanical and bears only on the "why"; it is a fairly straightforward corollary of the *Ethics:* a "natural" process is by definition nonartistic. However, the other three answers are to conspicuously modern questions.

They are indeed modern questions in that they test concrete aspects of modern man's practical activity in order to evaluate their aesthetic value, whatever we may think of Joyce's answer. His condemnation of photography or of the artworks of the mentally unbalanced may disappoint the contemporary reader. But the very fact that such questions were raised indicates a genuine interest in the impact of modern technology on our culture (was not Joyce, after all, the first Irishman to try and open cinemas in Dublin less than a decade later?), as well as in the "subtle knots" described and investigated by contemporary psychology and psychiatry. As for his conservative acceptance of "houses, clothes, furniture, etc." as works of art, it no less remarkably reflects contemporary interests, and it echoes Bosanquet's approval of, and long quotations from, William Morris's lectures (Bosanquet, 95ff., 124ff., 454ff.). Neo-Hegelian Bosanquet had made it clear from the beginning that "the history of aesthetic theory . . . is a narrative which traces the aesthetic consciousness in its intellectual form of aesthetic theory, but never forgets that the central matter to be elucidated is the value of beauty for human life, no less as implied in practice than as explicitly recognized in reflection" (Bosanquet, 2).

Now those are also modern *questions* in a broad acceptation of the term: as part of a dialectic pattern, they are symptoms of a divided mind, typical of decadent or transitional periods. Such was Joyce's cultural situation, historically no less than psychologically. Again, Bosanquet provides an illuminating background to his inquiry, especially in his chapter 5, "Alexandrian and Greco-Roman Culture to the Reign of Constantine the Great": the period encapsulates the contradiction between the antique and the modern spirit. To put matters in a nutshell,

> whereas the antique spirit is single, the modern is divided. Tested therefore by the extreme of any abstract tendency, the modern spirit overpasses the antique; only the completeness and thoroughness, whether intellectual or imaginative or political and social, that marks the highest perfection of genius as of life, is for this very reason difficult of attainment in a "modern" period. . . . Thus we can understand how the culture of the "decadence" was at once more "objective" and more "subjective," more individualistic yet more alive to humanity as a whole, more ascetic yet more romantic, than that of the preceding age. (Bosanquet, 80).

Bosanquet's analysis of decadence could not but help Joyce to clarify his own subjective position. It came very close indeed to formulating his own crisis and aesthetic program:

> The culture of this age is distinguished from that which preceded it by subjectivity and individualism [and] we must understand that we are speaking of a complex modern subjectivity, and a relative modern individualism. It is a subjectivity which in its skeptical divorce from metaphysics throws itself into materialistic science as one complement, if it falls into mystical intuitionism as another; it is an individualism which separates itself from the narrow selfishness of the tribe or city no less than from its limited self-sacrifice, and in busying itself with the problems of reasonable pleasure is never far from the aspirations of religious asceticism. (Bosanquet, 85)

Leaving aside some specific remarks of Bosanquet's that might easily be brought to bear on the works of Joyce, such as his presentation of "technical terms and distinctions . . . that have descended . . . to modern times," or his insistence on the growing "sympathy with townlife" in the period, which is no less reminiscent of *Dubliners* and *Finnegans Wake* than of *Ulysses,* we shall concentrate on two observations.

The first and more general observation brings together a number of hints by Bosanquet to the effect that the period in question paved the way to a *new, modern concept of the subject:* "It is only the simple truth if we say that no speculative thinker of at all the same caliber as Aristotle existed again before the time of Descartes" (Bosanquet, 77). And again: "Augustine, at the close of the fourth [century], was to announce the distinctively modern principle of a certainty implied in intellectual doubt" (Bosanquet, 78). The consequences of this revolution were far-reaching, as "the problem of practice emerged in a new perspective and proportion," thus giving birth to "a new personal ethic" (Bosanquet, 82).

Such hints gain even more significance when set side by side with Bosanquet's insistence on a new concept of "materialistic science." And they may be extended to bear on the domain of literature: for the period was one in which the notion of character, first adumbrated by Aristotle in terms of *ethos* and *pathos,* was the object of reexamination, especially in the teaching of Theophrastus (Bosanquet, 79, 82). The epistemological implications of Joyce's research are quite consonant with Bosanquet's picture of Alexandrian decadence as anticipating modern culture: in his time, too, in a context that was supposed to savor of at least literary decadence, new concepts of man, of science, and of the community were, if not born yet, at least in gestation, or perhaps even, as Joyce himself wrote in one of his most direct confessions, "in travail." They could be referred, *mutatis mutandis,* to their slow and painful proleptic emergence in the late Renaissance and seventeenth century.

The second and final observation bears on Plotinus, "the last great Hellenic thinker," presented by Bosanquet from the outset as having "broken the bonds of ancient theory concerning the beautiful," symmetrically with the Augustinian *cogito* (Bosanquet, 78). Now, without anticipating unduly the next chapter, I must stress once more the Neoplatonic strain in young Joyce's theorizing, perceptible in his specific use of Aquinas. Indeed, Neoplatonism, or at least Plotinus, could be thought to be relevant to the modern artist, not simply because they were then fashionable in Dublin, but also because they did harmonize substantially with modern preoccupations: it "almost succeeded in grasping the fundamental idea of *evolution;* viz. that *derivative is not necessarily the inferior*" (Bosanquet, 85, italics mine), and, more generally,

> although [Neoplatonism] was . . . a half-system, being fundamentally mystical, that is to say, having lost faith in life and science, and being compelled for that reason to yield the scepter to Christianity, yet just as Christianity, although a concrete principle of life, constantly fell into repellent one-sidedness, so Neoplatonism, though not a concrete principle of life, was profound enough to inspire a great mind for a time with a comprehensive faith in *the reasonableness of reality.* (Bosanquet, 99, italics mine)

We may discover soon that another great mind in turn was inspired by Plotinus with a comparable faith that helped him to come to terms with the temptation of the mystical.

CHAPTER SIX

The Pola Notebook and Aquinas

·

THE so-called Pola Notebook is Joyce's last purely theoretical production, though several sentences from it are repeated verbatim in either *Stephen Hero* or *A Portrait of the Artist.*

Two of the Pola Notebook's fragments are put under the aegis of epigraphs from Saint Thomas Aquinas, which invites us to try to assess briefly Joyce's debt to scholastic philosophy, all the more so as external evidence, namely, *Stephen Hero,* shows that Joyce's whole argument is oriented by a third, silent reference to the same author. Father William T. Noon has masterfully gathered and sifted the evidence, and it would be futile to paraphrase his study. I will confine myself to another task: that of reconstructing Joyce's general argument, without considering whether he was a good Thomist, wholesale or in detail, a question that Father Noon thoroughly examined.

Father Noon has made it clear that Joyce had, properly speaking, no systematic training in scholastic philosophy. And there is some biographical truth in Stephen's statement in *A Portrait of the Artist* that "the lore which he was believed to pass his days brooding upon so that it had rapt him from the companionships of youth was only a garner of slender sentences from Aristotle's poetics and psychology and a *Synopsis Philosophiae Scholasticae ad Mentem Divi Thomae*" (*PA,* 176–77). Contrary to general opinion, this *Synopsis* is not fictional; it has actual bibliographic existence,[1] and Joyce almost certainly came

100

across it in Paris and consulted it in Bibliothèque Sainte-Geneviève. There is no indication that he bought a copy of it, at a time when he could barely make ends meet, and no internal evidence suggests that he used it extensively despite a few verbal echoes. Its mention in *A Portrait of the Artist* (and nowhere else) indicates that Joyce aims at emphasizing Stephen's intellectual snobbery, and it may carry the additional profit of a private joke: the book, a mechanical digest for seminary students, is not only an outline of Thomistic philosophy but also a detailed and systematic criticism of lay philosophies, especially modern ones; it may also be a personal memento of the Paris episode, which could not be evoked directly in *A Portrait of the Artist,* because the book could hardly admit of a false start, but stage only one, decisive departure from Dublin.

These restrictions should not lead us to underestimate Joyce's acquaintance with Aquinas. I share Father Noon's view that, although Joyce probably "made little formal study of St. Thomas' works . . . the chances are that his curiosity and his independent desire to check and to interpret sources for himself led him to do some work privately on the text of Aquinas in an informal way," and I also agree that he is likely to have consulted the *Revue néo-scolastique.*[2] We should therefore pay special attention to the context in which Aquinian quotations appear, whether in Joyce's writings or in his assumed source books.

The Pola Notebook, although it will be discovered precisely to aim at a (re)definition of the conditions of *pulchritudo,* ostensibly focuses on an analysis of the act of aesthetic apprehension, the best-known formulation of which is found in *A Portrait of the Artist* (211–12). However, the approach here is meticulously analytical and is signposted by two epigraphs from Aquinas.

The first of them, *Bonum est in quod tendit appetitus,* prefixed to the first fragment, is a quotation, in slightly modified form, from the *Summa Contra Gentiles,* book 3, chapter 3, "Quod omne agens agit propter bonum," in which Aquinas develops the opening statement from the Latin translation of the *Nichomachean Ethics,* "Bonum est quod omnia appetunt," or, to give a fuller context: "Every art and every investigation *[methodos]*, and likewise every practical pursuit or undertaking, seems to aim at some good: hence it has been well said that the Good is That at which all things aim."[3] This sets the key for the whole Pola Notebook, whose line of investigation is definitely *ethical* and oriented in the first place by the Aristotelian-Aquinian problematics. Let us begin with Aristotle's next pronouncements: "A certain variety is to be observed among the ends at which the arts and sciences aim: in some cases the activity of practising the art is itself the end, whereas in others the end is some product over and above the mere exercise of the art; and in the arts whose ends *[télé]* are certain things beside the practice *[praxeis]* of the arts themselves, these products are essentially superior in value to the activities *[energeion]*." The observation enables us to understand Joyce's distinction between the "activities" involved in apprehension, which he examines in his second fragment, and the *act* of apprehension, which is the proper subject matter of the third, final fragment, and constitutes a stepping stone toward a theoretical synthesis with Joyce's own experience of "epiphany": from which it will be made quite clear that this act is not of the nature of an *energeia* (as kinetic), but teleologically oriented toward (static) "satisfaction," or *jouissance,* as distinct from pleasure.

Fragment two, also under the aegis of Aquinas ("Pulchra sunt quae visa placent"), analyses the aesthetic art culminating in satisfaction, or *jouissance,* into its component "activities" described as merely "pleasant." As early as fragment one, this analysis aims at presenting "the desirable" in its "most persistent" modes as "spiritual appetites" susceptible to be appeased by the "most satisfying *relations* [of the intelligible, of the sensible]," and formulating a teleology of desire which disentangles it from its physical associations and presents it in terms of intelligible structure. Now, of course, this insistence on discursive, intelligible structure is quite consonant with Aquinas's conception of the Beautiful as concerning the cognitive faculty, and Joyce (after Bosanquet, 147) follows Aquinas's lead: "Pulchrum autem respicit vim cognoscitivam: pulchra enim dicuntur ea quae visa placent."

Joyce obvious exploits Bosanquet's presentation of Aquinas's view of symbolism:

> Although St. Thomas makes the senses the direct bearers of this affinity [between the percipient and the perceived]—"the senses are charmed with things duly proportioned, as analogous to themselves ('Sicut in sibi similibus')"—yet he clearly adopts the derivation of all beauty from God, and gives, like Plotinus, the first rank to the sense of sight because of its affinity to the intellect.
>
> Thus we may conclude that symmetry is beautiful, for him as for his predecessors, because *symbolic of reason* and divinity; but he does not, any more than they, follow Plotinus in the demand for life and expression as something more than symmetry. (Bosanquet, 147–48, italics mine)

From this follows Joyce's description of "the activity of cognition or simple perception" as the first phase of the "act of apprehension." As for the second, "the activity of recognition," Joyce's analysis is slightly more complex, as it echoes Aristotelian *anagnorisis,* as expounded by Butcher (201):

> Recognition, as the name indicates, is a change from ignorance to knowledge, producing love or hate between the persons destined by the poet for good or bad fortune. The best form of recognition is coincident with a Reversal of the Situation, as in the Oedipus. There are indeed other forms. *Even inanimate things of the most trivial kind may in a sense be objects of recognition.* Again, we may recognize or discover whether a person has done a thing or not. But the recognition which is most intimately connected with the plot and action is, as we have said, the recognition of persons. This recognition, combined with Reversal, will produce either pity or fear. (*Poet.* XI.2–4. Butcher, 41, italics mine)

This passage illuminates much of Joyce's theorizing. Aristotle's extension of recognition to "inanimate things of the most trivial kind" prefigures Joyce's insistence on triviality in the epiphanic experience (*SH,* 211–13 passim). In the same way, the discovery of "whether a person has done a thing or not" is of the order of a "sudden spiritual manifestation" (*SH,* 211–13 passim), or "betrayal," to use Joyce's favorite concept. Again, his extensive use of the word "soul" (e.g., "the soul of the commonest object," *SH,* 213) is not a slip of the pen, but the deliberate assertion of his epistemological position. Hence also his inclusion of "the most hideous object" in the category of the beautiful, a question that traverses Bosanquet's whole *A History of Aesthetic,* as connected with "the general theory of pleasure and pain" and the problem of "the psychical connection between content and expression" (Bosanquet, 467); here Aquinas might have been quoted with pertinence: "Aliqua imago dicitur esse pulchra si perfecte repraesentat rem, quamvis turpem" (S.T. I.q.39, a.8, ad 2m, a passage to which we will have to revert).

Lastly, attention must be drawn to Aristotle's emphasis on persons as agents, and its special impact when combined with Reversal. On the face of it, Joyce hardly seems to follow Aristotle—that is, unless we try to understand what he means by his definition of the activity of recognition as "an activity of decision": the ethical *act* involved in *anagnorisis.* Joyce, though not mentioning "persons" at this point, is paving the way toward a problematics of Persons as interrelated, as the locus of symbolic exchanges, thus delineating the Real as Wholly Other: *vide* Aristotle's arch-example of the *Oedipus . . .* no less than Trinitarian theology.

In other words, Joyce is at pains to demonstrate that relations and structure, as conceived by him, have the widest extension possible. *The ultimate import of the matter is ontological,* over and above the methodological, and this is where he comes across difficulties as regards Truth and the Real. Hence his search for solutions through practical applications of the Trinitarian model. His choice of the ontological is patent in his subsuming of the Beautiful to the Good. The lines immediately preceding the above Aquinian quotation make the nature of the choice quite clear:

> Dicendum quod pulchrum et bonum *in subjecto* [i.e., ontologically] quidem sunt idem, quia super eamdem rem fundantur, scilicet super formam: et propter hoc, bonum laudatur ut pulchrum. Sed *ratione* [i.e., methodologically] differunt. Nam bonum proprie respicit appetitum: est enim bonum quod omnia appetunt. Et ideo habet rationem finis: nam appetitus est quasi qui-

dam motus ad rem. Pulchrum autem respicit vim cognoscitivam: pulchra enim dicuntur quae visa placent (S.T. I.i.q.5, a.4, italics mine).

Joyce deliberately ignores the distinction and there lies his *coups de force*. He couples Truth and Beauty, which is totally illegitimate in Thomistic philosophy, as Father Noon points out: "Aquinas in his discussion of beauty never uses the Platonic formula, *splendor veri*. In Thomistic metaphysics, at any rate, the true is always predicated analogously, just as *ens,* or being, is."[4] What he does here, then in *Stephen Hero* and finally, in modified form in *A Portrait of the Artist,* is to identify Thomistic metaphysics and aesthetics, to "apply" such a philosophy to his aesthetic experience. His final section, "The Act of Apprehension," which presents this experience explicitly and insistently in terms of "practical" aesthetic philosophy, sums it up in a ternary structure of cognition, recognition, and satisfaction. He thus prefigures a Trinitarian *analogon* to be spelt out in *Stephen Hero* a few months later, when Stephen prefixes his description of the epiphany with the key Aquinian tag he had already used as a weapon against the President of the University (*SH*, 96): "You know [Stephen is addressing Lynch] what Aquinas says: The three things requisite for beauty are, integrity, a wholeness, symmetry and radiance. Some day I will expand that sentence into a treatise" (*SH*, 212). What follows immediately is a mere rewriting of the Pola Notebook:

> Consider the performance of your own mind when confronted with any object, hypothetically beautiful. Your mind to apprehend that object divides the entire universe into two parts, the object, and the void which is not the object. To apprehend it you must lift it away from everything else: and then you perceive that it is one integral thing, that is *a* thing. You recognise its integrity. . . . That is the first quality of beauty: it is declared in a simple sudden synthesis of the faculty which apprehends. What then? Analysis then. The mind considers the object in whole and in part, in relation to itself and to other objects, examines the balance of its parts, contemplates the form of the object, traverses every cranny of the structure. So the mind receives the impression of the symmetry of the object. The mind recognizes

that the object is in the strict sense of the word, a *thing*, a definitely constituted entity. (*SH*, 212)

Joyce's treatment of the third "activity," however, is more specific and articulate, and it will be discovered to be more deceptive as well as more revealing. It is more revealing in that he comments his position as regards *claritas* (radiance):

> Now for the third quality. For a long time I couldn't make out what Aquinas meant. He uses a figurative word (a very unusual thing for him) but I have solved it. *Claritas* is *quidditas*. After the analysis which discovers the second quality the mind makes the only logically possible synthesis and discovers the third quality. This is the moment which I call epiphany. First we recognize that the object is *one* integral thing, then we recognize that it is an organized composite structure, a *thing* in fact: finally, when the relation of the parts is exquisite, when the parts are adjusted to the special point, we recognize that it is *that* thing which it is. Its soul, its whatness, leaps to us from the vestment of its appearance. The soul of the commonest object, the structure of which is so adjusted, seems to us radiant. The object achieves its epiphany. (*SH*, 213)

In a sense Joyce admits that, by interpreting a figurative word, he has solved not only a linguistic, semantic problem but also an ontological mystery, that of the Trinity. For Aquinas's dictum is really part of a discussion on the attributes of the Three Persons: "Ad pulchritudinem tria requiruntur. Primo quidem integritas, sive perfectio; (quae enim diminuta sunt, hoc ipso turpia sunt), et debita proportio, sive consonantia; et iterum claritas; unde quae habent colorem nitidum, pulchra esse dicuntur." Aquinas here is wondering why Saint Hilary considers *aeternitas* as the attribute of the Father, *species*, or image, as that of the Son, and *usus*, enjoyment, or *jouissance*, as that of the Holy Spirit. The Son can be said to be *Species* insofar as he resembles the Father perfectly; and such a perfect Image is no less than uncreated Beauty. Human experience of the beauty of art *objects* is an *analogon*, a similitude of such transcendent beauty.

Joyce's *coup de force* precisely lays in his "logical . . . synthesis," in his conflation of *claritas* and *quidditas*, or whatness.

And, as Annie Tardits points out, "the presence of the essence of the object is tantamount to a presence of essence as object."[5] Now, the whole history of the Christian church, and of Christian culture at large, the gradual building up of its dogma and of its culture, developed against a background of heresies centering on the problem of image versus substance (*ousia, essentia*). It is no wonder then that Joyce's present heretical position is to be developed later on in *Ulysses,* with special reference to Sabellianism. Beyond Aquinas looms a much broader horizon.

·

ONCE again Bosanquet may be our guide at this point. Not merely because, by giving chapter and verse for the Aquinian texts on beauty (Bosanquet, 147–48), he may have stimulated Joyce decisively, but more substantially on account of the broad historical context he keeps weaving; this context has already been sketched in the previous discussions of symbolism. The doctrine that Plotinus defended was presented as the fountainhead of medieval and, beyond it, modern aesthetic thought and practice. On the metaphysical level, he asserted the rights of symbolism, his position being that "the arts do not simply imitate the visible, but go back to the reasons *[logous]* from which nature comes; . . . they create much out of themselves, and add to that which is defective, as being themselves in possession of beauty; since Pheidias did not create his Zeus after any perceived pattern, but made him such as he would be if Zeus deigned to appear to mortal eyes" (Bosanquet, 113). On the ethical level, "beauty comes to be regarded as a direct expression of reason in sense by way of aesthetic semblance only and is therefore *co-ordinate with morality* and not subordinate to it" (Bosanquet, 115, italics mine). As a consequence, on the aesthetic level, "the identification of beauty with symmetry, or unity in variety . . . is broken down when the beauty of art ceases to be subordinate to the standards of ordinary reality" (Bosanquet, 116), which leads to the famous dictum, "Beauty is rather a light that plays over the symmetry of things than the symmetry itself."

Now, the disintegration of ancient thought that Plotinus initiated contributed to generate the modern mind, even though, as Bosanquet admits, one must wait until Shakespeare or Goethe to meet "an aesthetic mood which is symbolic like that of the middle age, but without its arbitrary mysticism, and un-artificial, like that of classical Greece, but free from its imitative naturalism" (Bosanquet, 119). What then characterizes the Middle Ages is a "remarkable circuit of theory" beginning with the successors of Plotinus and "ending with a complete rec-ognition of a more significant beauty as the manifestation of the Divine both through art and nature in the age of St. Fran-cis, St. Thomas, Dante and Giotto" (Bosanquet, 131–32). Of special importance are phases through which the Christian dogma passed before its ultimate formulation in scholastic phi-losophy, such as Augustinian theology, the Arian crisis, and the system of Scotus Erigena. The latter, whose translation into Latin of the Pseudo-Dionysius (himself "saturated with the ideas of Plotinus") was a major influence on Aquinas's aes-thetic opinions, laid down "as essential to beauty that the vis-ible creation shall be apprehended as a revelation of the glory of God, and therefore apart from the relation of sensuous de-sire . . . , [applying] this sense of rationality to the whole world through and through, not merely to art nor to the choicer parts of nature; thus manifesting that conviction of universal significance which lies at the root both of modern science and of modern art" (Bosanquet, 143), the first step being the dis-placement of the *kalon* of the Ancients by medieval *pulchritudo*.

The Pola Notebook is, to all appearances, the ultimate relic of Joyce's aesthetic. It testifies to the breadth of his initial proj-ect, which was to build up an entire system encompassing an-cient and modern conceptions about art and the beautiful, a system, though, that could accommodate his "epiphany." The *Summa Theologica* that he dipped into at this stage is indeed one of those models that have haunted Western consciousness for centuries, from Aristotle to Hegel, among others; and no less than Spinoza's *Ethics* and Descartes's *Meditations* are im-pregnated by such an implicit ambition of total summation, as has been pointed out.[6] That this summation, though based in Joyce's as in Descartes's case, on the assumptions of modern science, is imaginary, in the Lacanian sense, is confirmed by Joyce's fascination with its synoptic possibilities. I have selected two major sample pages from the *Synopsis Philsophiae Scolasticae*. One (p. 29 in *Cosmologia*) presents scholastic *Systema materiae et formae*, of particular interest to us because the concept of *materia prima* seems to have held a pivotal position in Joyce's projected system (*CW,* 134: "That idea [in Bruno's philosophy] of an ultimate principle, spiritual, indifferent, universal, related to any soul or to any material thing [see *PA,* 215], as the Materia Prima of Aquinas is related to any material thing, unwarranted as it may seem in the view of critical philosophy, has yet a distinct value for the historian of religious ecstasies"). The other (p. 43 in *Dynamilogia*) presents *Diversae functiones intellectus,* that is, *judicium, ratio, conscientia, memoria intellectiva,* which may have offered Joyce operative distinctions and prospective lines of analysis.

But imaginary constructions do not offer only narcissistic satisfactions, they may also reveal the lack, or the flaw, in the subject's image of himself, in Joyce's case, an intellectual image.[7] Indeed, the Pola Notebook contains the contradictions he failed to negotiate and upon which his aesthetic was to founder: image versus symbol, nature versus grace, essence versus object, ethics versus ontology. . . .

ARTICULUS I — CORPORA INANIMA

Essentia corporum.

2. Atomismus chimicus.

1. Expositio.
: Corpora sunt simplicia vel composita; haec constituuntur atomis vel moleculis corporum simplicium, actualiter in eis existentium. — Tongiorgi, Secchi, etc.

2. Appretiatio. (*Atomismus chimicus est saltem incompletus.*)
 1. Nam falsò fundatur. — Etenim quaestio de principiis essentialibus non est physica (de factis), sed metaphysica (de essentiâ). —
 2. Nam non explicat quaestionem (seu est incompletus).
   1. Quoad corpora simplicia.
      1. Etenim non explicat quomodò habeant aliquid commune et aliquid distinctum.
      2. Etenim non explicat quomodò habeant activitatem et extensionem.
   2. Quoad corpora composita : — Etenim non potest explicare an elementa remaneant in eis *actu* vel *virtute* tantùm.

3. Dynamismus.

1. Expositio. — Corpora componuntur viribus seu principiis inextensis et activis. — Wolfius, Boscowichius, Kantius.

2. Refutatio. (*Dynamismus est falsus.*)
 1. Nam non explicat diversitatem substantialem corporum.
 2. Nam non explicat extensionem. — Etenim *intercalà supposita* inter monades sunt impossibilia, monades non producerent extensionem, quae non dat extensionem, cum non possent *agere*; si agerent, adesset tantùm *relatio* inter monades, quae non dat extensionem. — Aliunde extensio non exurgit ex *collectione monadum*, nec est in *sensatione* alicujus vis resistentiae.

4. Systema materiae et formae.
(*Th. Systema materiae et formae est admittendum.*)

1. Prenotanda.
 1. Formula generalis : — Essentia corporum constituitur duplici elemento : uno passivo et indeterminato (materia prima), altero activo et determinante (forma substantialis).
 2. De materia.
   1. Quid sit in genere : — Subjectum ex quo, — in quo, — circa quod aliquid fit.
   2. Materia prima.
      1. Negative : — Id quod neque est quid, neque quantum, neque quale, neque aliquid eorum quibus ens determinatur.
      2. Positive : — Subjectum in quo forma recipitur, quod idem remanet in omnibus corporibus, et ex quo promanat eorum extensio.
 3. De forma.
   1. Quid sit.
      1. Quoad nomen : — Sic vocatur propter praestantiam sui muneris.
      2. Quoad rem : — Id quod rem ad certum essendi modum determinat.
   2. Quotuplex forma.
   3. De formâ substantiali informanti : — Est actus primus materiae, — seu principium ex quo compositum habet suam speciem et activitatem.
 4. Relationes materiae et formae.
   1. Quoad essentiam : — *Altera ab alterâ completur* (specificatio, — individuatio).
   2. Quoad existentiam.
      1. *Materia nequit esse sine formâ* : — Nam non habet speciem.
      2. *Forma (non subsistens) nequit esse sine materiâ* : — Nam non habet individuationem.
 5. Productio formae.
   1. In composito creato : — Fit cum materiâ ex nihilo.
   2. In composito generato : — Fit per *eductionem de potentiâ materiae* : — seu agens product formam *praesuppositâ materiâ* ut principio coadjuvante.
 6. Nullum corpus, nulla pars materiae de novo creatur.
 7. *Mutationes substantiales realiter existunt in rerum naturâ* : — Nam realiter sunt mutationes quae manifestant novas proprietates omninò diversas et saepe oppositas prioribus.

2. Solutio.
 1. Auctoritate.
   1. Philosophicâ : — Plato, Aristoteles, Cicero, S. Augustinus, S. Thomas, omnes Scolastici, Suarezius, etc.
   2. Theologicâ : — Dogma unionis substantialis animae cum corpore. — Sacra Eucharistia, in quâ extensio manet sine substantiâ.
 2. Nam rectè explicat duas proprietates corporum : extensionem et activitatem, — Etenim supponit *duo principia*, unum passivum et commune (fons extensionis), alterum activum et determinatum (fons activitatis), — quae *duo* requiruntur propter diversitatem notarum extensionis et activitatis.
 3. Nam admitti in rebus †) subjectum realiter existens, receptivum formarum (materiam primam), — 2) principium determinativum hujus potentiae materialis (formam substantialem). — *Prob. maj.* Ex 7° praenotamine.

3. Scholion : Principium individuationis.
 1. Sensus quaestionis : — Unde substantia in suo esse individui constituatur?
 2. Principia. — Id in quo differt ab alio debet esse aliquid intrinsecum, substantiale.
 3. Diverse sententiae.
   1. Quoad composita materiâ et formâ.
      1. Est *materia signata quantitate* (seu subjecta determinatis dimensionibus). Alioquin esset forma (quae est fons unitalis specificae), vel materia sola (quae est nimis indeterminata).
      2. Hoc evenit in homine : Anima est principium formale specificans, — corpus determinatum definita quantitate est principium individuationis (non principium personalitatis).
   2. Quoad substantias completas simplices.
      1. Est forma : — Nam in illis est unicum principium intrinsecum.
      2. Corollarium : — Quodcumque individuum est *species distincta* : — Nam habet formam propriam et distinctam formam.

2. Diversæ functiones intellectus.

1. Judicium.

1. **Intellectio est simul passiva et activa.**
   1. Prænotanda.
      1. Errores.
         1. Plato, etc. : — Species rerum sunt innatæ menti nostræ, quæ est purè passiva.
         2. Transcendentales Germani : — Objecta cognitionis ab animâ creantur vel construuntur. — Intellectus est purè activus.
         3. Henricus Gandavensis, Ockamus, multi recentes : — Statim ac phantasma obviam fit intellectui, iste ex vi sibi insitâ efformat ideam rerum.
      2. Duplex potentia activa.
         1. Una efficit totum suum objectum.
         2. Altera in illud agit transmutando et appropriando.
         - 1ª Pars : — Non est purè passiva. — Nam reddit intelligibile actuale, et exprimit verbum.
         - 2ª Pars : — Non est purè activa. — Nam hoc ducere ad Idealismum, — Nam intellectus haberet virtutem infinitam, — Etenim exercetur circa infinita objecta.
   2. Solutio.
      1. Ratione principii immediati, seu potentiæ.
      2. Ratione objecti.
      3. Ratione multiplicitatis actuum.
      4. Ratione perfectionis.
2. **Differentia inter intellectionem et sensationem.**
   1. Intellectus dat cognitionem perfectam.
   2. Sensatio dat cognitionem imperfectam.
3. **Corollaria.**

2. Ratio.

1. *Actus proprius intellectûs nostri est judicium.* — Nam est attingere veritatem non unico conspectu, sed comparando ideas inter se, et posteà pronuntiando circa earum convenientiam vel repugnantiam. — Etenim cum actus intellectûs imperfectissimi.
2. *Judicium non est actus voluntatis* (contra Cartesium). — Nam habet pro objecto verum ut verum.
3. *Judicia instinctiva non oriuntur, sed omne judicium est comparativum.*
   - 1ª Pars : — Nam essent judicia quæ intellectus pronuntiaret ex solo impulsu naturæ, sine præviâ relationis terminorum cognitione.
   - 2ª Pars : — Nam pronuntiatur circa relationem duarum notionum ex præviâ earumdem cognitione.

1. Ratio speculativa et ratio practica.
   1. Quid sint.
      - 1ª Quæ sistit in idearum contemplatione.
      - 2ª Quæ applicat cognitionem ad opus.
   2. Differentia.
      1. Prænotandum : — Error Alberti magni, et Kantii : — Sunt duæ potentiæ distinctæ.
      2. Solutio. : {*Ratio speculativa et ratio practica non sunt potentiæ distinctæ.* Nam non habent objecta formaliter diversa.}
2. Intellectus et ratio.
   1. Quid sint.
      - 1ª Quo mens percipit principia per se et immediate nota.
      - 2ª Quâ discurrit ex notis ad ignota.
   2. Differentia.
      1. Prænotandum : — Error Kantii.
      2. Solutio. : {*Intellectus et ratio non sunt potentiæ distinctæ.* — Nam objecta (omne ens intelligibile) et actus (plus minusve perfectus) non sunt specifice diversa.}
3. Ratio superior et ratio inferior.
   1. Quid sint.
      - 1ª Quæ intendit æternis.
      - 2ª Quæ intendit temporalibus.
   2. Differentia. : *Non sunt potentiæ distinctæ.* — Nam non habent objecta formaliter diversa.

3. Conscientia.

1. Quid sit et quotuplex.
   1. Quid sit : — Functio intellectûs quâ anima percipit operationes et affectiones spirituales et præsentes.
   2. Quotuplex.
      1. Habitualis.
      2. Actualis.
      - 1. Quoad nomen : — Habitus, dispositio.
      - 2. Quoad rem : — Quâ mens non se actu cognoscit, sed expedita est ad se actu cognoscendum.
      - — Quâ mens seipsam cognoscit eò quod se agentem percipit.
2. Natura.
   Th. : *Conscientia non est potentia specialis distincta ab intellectu.*
   1. Prænotandum : — Error Reidii, etc.
   2. Solutio.
      1. Nam habet idem objectum formale ac intellectus, — Etenim subjectum cogitans et ejus affectiones sunt aliquid immateriale ac intelligibile.
      2. Nam est vis quâ intellectus potest in se reflecti.
3. Objectum.
   1. Objectum directum.
      Th. : *Actus intellectûs et voluntatis sunt objectum directum conscientiæ.*
   2. Objectum indirectum.
      Th. : *Operationes sensitivæ et vitales non sunt objectum directum; subjectum cogitans est objectum indirectum conscientiæ.*
      - 1ª Pars : — Nam actus intellectûs est id quod conscientia primò et directè percipit, — Etenim intellectus, reflectendo supra seipsum, primò et directè percipit suos proprios actus.
      - 2. Nam actus voluntatis est intelligibilior in intellectu, — Etenim nihil volitum quin præcognitum.
      - 1ª Pars : — Nam non sunt aliquid immateriale et intelligibile.
      - 2ª Pars.
         1. Solutio. : {Nam est perceptum propter suam unionem cum objecto directè cognito, — Etenim intellectus, percipiens se agentem, percipit principium et subjectum operationis.}
         2. Scholion : — Subjectum cogitans apprehenditur solum in suâ existentiâ.
4. Duratio actus conscientiæ.
   Th. : *Conscientia actualis non semper exercetur; habitualis est semper actualiter in intellectu.*
   - 1ª Pars : — Nam est operatio quâ cognoscimus per reflexionem actus intellectûs nostri. — *Prob. maj.* — Nam intellectus non semper agit, nec semper attendimus ad ejus actus.
   - 2ª Pars : — Nam est dispositio ad se actu cognoscendum.

4. Memoria intellectiva.

1. Quid sit : — Est intellectus quatenus conservat, et recognoscit præteritos actus intellectûs et voluntatis. — Etenim hæc operatio est conservatio specierum intelligibilium, et recognitio earum ut prius cognitarum.
2. Natura.
   Th. : *Memoria non est potentia distincta ab intellectu.*
   — Nam non habet operationem specificè diversam ab operatione intellectûs, ...

Conclusion

·

Science and the aesthetic ideal . . . meet in their common exaggeration of the value of truth, more precisely in their common belief that truth is *in*estimable, *un*criticizable.
FRIEDRICH NIETZSCHE, *The Genealogy of Morals,* 3

WE MUST start over again from Joyce's paradox. On the one hand, Joyce is objectively the major innovator in the realm of modern writing, and seems to insist, at the outset of his career, on formulating the principles of this new writing, on demonstrating that he is the model "new man of letters," as well as the modern Newman. On the other hand, he clearly indicates that his major references are to established authorities, particularly Aristotle and Aquinas. Now this paradox should not blind us to the fact that it reflects, though conceals, underlying contradictions on which his project actually foundered, but which gave new impetus to his writing.

Joyce was undoubtedly a child of his age, open to contemporary influences, whether positive, as paths or simply suggestions to be followed, or negative, as "whetstones" (to use the phrase he applied to his brother Stanislaus), or both.

Among these influences was the latest movement in the British Isles, aestheticism and the so-called aesthetic tradition, which was leaving open the field for intellectual speculation as well as ethical choices. Such influences manifest themselves out of a very wide horizon, and they are difficult to pinpoint, still more to assess. Walter Pater may be a relative exception here. Joyce read him, as could be expected, and certainly felt he was closest to him on account of their common interest in the

112

broader perspective of the Hegelian system. For both of them, "impressionism" was not enough. But Joyce's attitude may be said to be symmetrical to Pater's. The latter's general, philosophical conception is unitive (as Joyce's, too, was for a time). His vision of history tends to be more affirmative than dialectal; a substantive acquaintance with European culture at large is for him a given and a precondition of aesthetic production and criticism.

This is apparent in his conception of *transitional* periods, a notion Joyce adopted in his early texts.[1] To him, the Renaissance was of special importance: "The essence of humanism is that belief . . . that nothing which has ever interested living men and women can wholly lose its vitality—no language they have spoken, no oracle beside which they have hushed their voices, no dream which has once been entertained by actual human minds, nothing about which they have ever been passionate, or expended time and zeal."[2]

As Wolfgang Iser points out, Pater "differs radically from an ethically oriented cultural philosophy which conceived of the Renaissance as a major shift from the past, giving birth to a new ideal of man." His philosophy is one of reconciliation (and his conception of myth is archetypal). This is especially apparent with one of his concepts, "mood," which Joyce, after W. B. Yeats, thought congenial to his theorizing (*SH,* 32, 162; *PA,* 67, 78, 168, 176, 215); and "Moods" is the actual title he gave to his first, abortive collection of poems written in 1896. Here is an illustration from Pater's *Renaissance:*

> To him [Botticelli], as to Dante, the scene, the color, the outward image or gesture, comes with all its incisive and importunate reality; but awakes in him, moreover, by some subtle law of its own structure, a mood which it awakes in no one else, of which it is the double, or repetition, and which it clothes, that all may share it, with visible circumstance [See Joyce's "The lyrical form is in fact the simplest verbal vesture of an instant of emotion," *PA,* 214]. . . . So just what Dante scorns as unworthy alike of heaven and hell, Botticelli accepts, that middle world in which men take no side in great conflicts, and decide no great causes, and make great refusals. He thus sets for himself the lim-

its within which art, undisturbed by any moral ambition, does its most sincere and surest work.[3]

However, Joyce's conception of the pictural and imaginative function differs from Pater's, which is also why the epiphany, despite similitudes, differs from Pater's, or for that matter from Yeats's, "mood." The epiphany does not find its justification in humanistic History, as Pater's "mood" and his "outward image" do. The epiphanic simile is ambiguous: as evocative of the starry dome, its connotation is immutablitity and the invariable recurrence of the Real; as unique phenomenon, it means a radical break and a new departure. It does not only evoke repetition, but as Difference, as the moment of writing per se, the rewriting of the heavenly Sign scribbled over the starry vault, it legitimates History, is its original legitimacy, being the signature in Nature verifying its origin in the Birth of the Son of Man. For the same reason, myth in this context does not justify writing, as it does with Pater; writing justifies myth by rewriting it: *Ulysses* is already looming through Joyce's scribblings (remember the close of "James Clarence Mangan": "The ancient gods, who are visions of the divine names, die and come to life many times"). Joyce's interminable "brooding" (a favorite word of his) on his experience in the epiphany is indeed on a wholly different track from Pater's. Joyce shows himself more than ready to confront and deal with, rather than sublimize, the impossibly horrible *jouissance,* of the kind that "James Clarence Mangan" had endeavored to convey by picturing extremes of pathetic abjection: a portrait that Pater's *Mona Lisa* as a paragon of Beauty was inadvertently devised to conceal.

Pater is only one item in his inventory of the intellectual material that could be borrowed from Joyce's contemporaries or near predecessors: Ruskin, Arnold,[4] Flaubert, Yeats, Wagner, Nietzsche, Symons, Ibsen, D'Annunzio, and so forth, not forgetting the *Encyclopedia Britannica.*[5] Bosanquet, and the general Hegelian perspective that had appealed to Pater before him, helped Joyce to find, if not a ready-made intellectual framework, at least a set of pertinent, manageable, and operative concepts and problems based on a coherent vision of the

Western tradition, and an analysis of modern subjectivity from the Renaissance to the contemporary period. Like Bosanquet, and perhaps following his example and advice, Joyce was alive to the actual conditions of modern art, to the specific problems he was facing, in short to the articulation of man with History in modern times. Hence his efforts at scrutinizing his subject in terms of the recently developed sciences of man: philology, the science of letters, but also medicine, psychiatry, and psychology, criminology, political economy, anthropology, and sociology. The perspective was genetic as well as historical:

> He doubled backwards into the past of humanity and caught glimpses of emergent art as one might have a vision of the plei-siosauros emerging from his ocean of slime. He seemed almost to hear the simple cries of fear and joy and wonder which are antecedent to all song, the savage rhythms of men pulling at the oar, to see the rude scrawls and the portable gods of men whose legacy Leonardo and Michelangelo inherit. And over this chaos of history and legend, of fact and supposition, he strove to draw out a line of order, the reduce the abysses of the past to order by a diagram. (*SH,* 33)

Joyce here effects another synthesis, between the suggestions of Plato concerning "primitive sounds," as reported by Bosanquet, and the most recent investigations of Yrjö Hirn.[6]

From Joyce's elaboration was due to emerge "a more veritably human tradition" (*SH,* 26), ultimately analyzed into a "literary tradition" as word conscious: "[Stephen] insisted on the importance of what he called the literary tradition. Words, he said, have a certain value in the literary tradition and a certain value in the market-place—a debased value. Words are simply receptacle for human thought: in the literary tradition they receive more valuable thoughts than they receive in the market-place" (*SH,* 27).

Joyce was enlisting the sciences of man for the greater glory of a tradition that was not only literary in the narrow sense but also philosophical and religious. Bosanquet and Butcher helped him in this tentative synthesis by emphasizing and mapping out the age-long conflict of imitation and symbolism. From the point of view of literary tradition, the Aristotelian formula, "imitation of nature" (*e tekhne mimeitai ten physin*) was as good a starting point as another; but it was of special pertinence to Joyce as focusing on two concepts and two aspects of existence that the epiphanic experience had questioned. Joyce's fascination with tabulation and the synoptic approach (*Synopsis Philosophiae Scolasticae . . . etc.*) is a symptom of a deeper personal *malaise:* one that has to do with the body as supported by what Lacan describes as the imaginary (function). One of the key passages in "James Clarence Mangan" can be interpreted along precisely those lines: "images herself in use": the image-making faculty and its production, the portrait of an ego, may be the subject's last resort, when confronted with hallucinatory *jouissance* and the Thing, *das Ding,*[7] his ultimate hope of staving off psychotic dissolution.[8]

In such a perspective, Joyce's identification as "Stephen," *the* Protomartyr, was a way of achieving fame through name (*renommée*) and, what is still more essential, of renaming himself *symbolically,* of existing spiritually. For Saint Stephen was the first martyr whose act of confessing his faith did not depend on a possible direct fascination with Christ as human figure, but was altogether the effect of symbolic transmission through the Word of the Apostles. So, if Joyce aimed at reconciliation, it was in a very special, problematical way rather than a dialectical one: one that was making room for, and indeed gave pride of place to, doubt of the Freudian type no less than of the Augustinian and Cartesian types.

At this point in this connection, I wish to suggest that his fleeting interest in occultisms has deeper roots than is usually estimated and was not merely ascribable to such external influences as Yeats's or AE's drawing his attention to Boehme, Swedenborg, and so forth. Characteristically, the 1904 "Portrait of the Artist" describes the artist as "the sensitive," a late-nineteenth-century vocable for "the medium." Spiritualism (the word itself is ambiguous) was a case of the dissociation of body and Word, when the medium allowed himself (or, more often than not, herself) to be traversed by the Word of the Other, and bodily convey what Lacan describes as "paroles imposées."[9] Typically, spiritualism raised a great interest among late-nineteenth-century scientists.[10]

Joyce's effort tended to translate and clarify the enigma of man's nature and God's love in grace in terms of *kinesis* (pleasure) and *stasis* (*jouissance*): but the aporia remained, even though it became a religious mystery. His averred reading of the *Summa Contra Gentiles* puts us on the track of his labyrinthine theoretical investigation, for there is to be met the difficult, often ambiguous synthesis of two conceptions of (human) nature, Aristotle's and Augustine's, the matter to be decided being whether reason may demonstrate that *natural desire* may give access to beatific vision. Aristotelian nature is an essence characterized by its own necessity, whereas Augustinian nature has, de facto, historically been constituted such as the creator chose to make it. The latter's native (Edenic) constitution implies a call to the supernatural and man's ordination to the beatific vision; the human soul is capable of grace, on account not of its essential nature but of its historical nature. Aquinas, though his use of the word "nature" is sometimes ambiguous, is quite clear about this: "Naturaliter animae est capax gratiae; eo enim ipso quod facta est ad imaginem Dei, capax est Dei per gratiam, ut Augustinus dixit" (S.T. I-II, qu.113 a.10). Throughout *Stephen Hero* and the *Portrait of the Artist* Stephen is seen confronting the enigma of nature, of human nature, which he sees as torn between the Augustinian sense of sin and grace and the Aristotelian necessity of self-realization. When Stephen says that he seeks a *bonum arduum* (*SH,* 180), his implicit reference to Aquinas (S.T. I-II, q.40, art.8) means that he *desires hope;* in other words, he fears to be a prey to despair, the sin against the Holy Ghost in Catholic theology, the only sin that cannot be forgiven and entails eternal damnation.

The themes of grace (see *PA,* 1904) and of love (God's and/ or the creature's) are merely another aspect of this division of the human subject. As Stephen says in the *Portrait of the Artist,* the mystery of the Holy Trinity was "easier of acceptance by his mind by reason of their august incomprehensibility" than "the simple fact that God had loved his soul from all eternity" (*PA,* 149). He also says, conversely: "I tried to love God. . . . It seems now I failed. It is very difficult. I tried to unite my will with the will of God instant by instant. In that I did not always fail. I could perhaps do that still" (*PA,* 240). This *potentia obe-*

dientialis, as Aquinas would say, stood Joyce in good stead. True, it was not to be travestied into mechanical obedience to passwords or worldly precepts, whether familial or Jesuitical. Hence the ambiguity of any call: was it addressed to a living subject, or to a potential object, "similiter atque senis bacculus," "loveless," "without joy . . . or hatred," supposed to be acting (for the word is hardly proper here) "perinde ac cadaver"?

Love also is unitive, even more so than science, as Aquinas in the *Summa Theologica* had reminded him: *"Amore est magis unitivus quam cognitio"* (S.T. I-II, qu.29, a. 1, ad 3m), adding elsewhere, however, that the love object is essentially twofold. The following passage from the *Summa Contra Gentiles,* which, it must be observed in passing, contains the passage about "the word known to all men" (*U,* 49, 581), Love, which Joyce was to omit (*U,* 195), deliberately or not, from the final version of *Ulysses,* gave him the clue:

> *Sciendum itaque quod, cum aliae operationes animae sint circa unum solum objectum, solus amor ad duo objecta ferri videtur. Per hoc enim quod intelligimus vel gaudemus, ad aliquod objectum aliqualiter nos habere opportet: amor vero aliquid alicui vult, hoc enim amare dicimur cui aliquod bonum volumus, secundum modum praedictum. Unde et ea quae concupiscimus, simpliciter quidem et proprie* desiderare *dicimur, non autem amare, sed potius nos ipos, quibus ea concupiscimus: et ex hoc ipsa per accidens et improprie dicuntur amari.* (*Summa Contra Gentiles* I, xci, "Quod in Deo sit amor")

This dual nature of the love object and the self-delusion that it may induce in the subject are what Lacan has described with his (untranslatable) concept of "objet a" (he says that it is his most original contribution to psychoanalysis). The epiphany, as presented in *Stephen Hero,* is the story of such self-delusion and failure: the failure to write a (love) story of subject and object except in the most abstract and disjointed theoretical terms. Here Joyce fails to put into practice his method as self-conscious, self-proclaimed scientist questioning "the dark recesses of consciousness," of man's "nature," to which nobody but himself, he seemed to say, does justice. Rather than an aesthetic, he was on his way to writing a new *Ethics,* only with a question mark added to Spinoza's dictum: *Deus, sive Natura?*

Hence the kinship of Joyce with such contemporary efforts as Nietzsche's: a questioning of man's categories and coordinates. Like him, and after Spinoza, he submits to vivisection the moral life of the modern subject: specifically what he calls "the moral history of [his] country"; in other words, the genealogy of Irish morals. Although his abandonment of the "science" of aesthetics is different from Nietzsche's contestation of science, "Jim the Overman," as he sometimes styled himself in letters to friends, was ineluctably led to subvert some age-old categories of the Western tradition. Brooding on the Mystery of the Holy Trinity (persons as relations in Love) led Joyce not to atheism or agnosticism, but to a conception of the Godhead that brought him in line with Spinoza's God: "invisible, refined out of existence, indifferent" (*PA,* 215), the Creator less as transcendent than as immanent agent. This is what Joyce may have read in a contemporary compendium of Nietzsche's thought: "Only in so far as the genius, in the act of artistic production, coalesces with the primordial artist of the world does he get a glimpse of the eternal essence of art; for in this state he is in a marvellous manner like the weird picture in the fairy-tale, which can at will turn its eyes and behold itself; he is now simultaneously subject and object, poet, actor, and spectator."[11]

No wonder that Joyce, like Nietzsche, found himself in harmony with Spinoza. Joyce's Aesthetic was obviously planned, like Spinoza's *Ethics,* and perhaps after it no less than after Aquinas, *more geometrico.* In the early months of 1903 in Paris, at the exact time he was working on the Paris Notebook, he proudly reported to Stanislaus (then to his mother) J. M. Synge's evaluation: "I told him part of my esthetic: he says I have a mind like Spinoza" (9 March 1903, *Letters,* 2:35). His description of the history of art in terms of "diagram" (*SH,* 31), his fascination with the concept of "gnomon" (*Dubliners,* Viking Critical Library, 9), his metaphor of "nicely-polished looking-glass" (*Letters,* 2) to describe his stance as writer of *Dubliners* (Spinoza's trade was glass and lens polishing), his eventual reference to the *Ethics* in the "Author's Notes" to *Exiles,* all point to a sort of mental identification with the post-Cartesian philosopher.[12]

Again such identification was basically, intrinsically imaginary: in terms of images rather than of discourse. Spinoza's method is "geometrical" in the sense of "demonstrative" rather than "based on geometric figures." Joyce was projecting himself into Spinoza's figure as intellectual (and heretical) figure as if what he needed was to *embody* his thought or, to use his own favorite phrase, to "image himself" in him. Again, this is symptomatic of an existential difficulty that Lacan points out in Joyce: how with him the imaginary (as distinct from symbolic and real) function, insofar as it is inseparably linked to the body, was particularly fragile, and susceptible to fail him in such moments of intensity as were recorded in the epiphanies. How could he repair such an existential flaw except through some special type of sublimation? He had to express in near-mystical terms his "very lively sense of spiritual obligations" (*Workshop,* 60), "that certitude which among men he had not found" (*Workshop,* 61). His sense of falling into an abyss and of redemption through language he interpreted and metaphorized in terms of Christian doctrine, but without being able, of course, to reconcile in his discourse the contradictory figures of Lucifer and Christ (or his representatives on earth).

For in the last analysis the aporia was the Word. The epiphany was Joyce's alpha and omega in his self-analysis as writer, and it has to be conceived as Janus-faced. On the one hand, it was indeed a *terminus ad quem,* the logical conclusion of his theoretical discourse, the culmination of his system (*SH,* 212–13), the ideally adequate production of the "prose of thought" foreshadowed by Bosanquet. It was the final word on and of the ultimate enunciation and Last Judgment, as the final speech act of the metalanguage he was planning to forge. As a mental structure based upon and expressive of his most vital constitution, the Aristotelian and scholastic systems and traditions that constituted "l'armature de ses pensées" (Lacan, "Séminaire Le Sinthome"), it was an absolutely vital *necessity:* "l'appensée," "la pensée" as "appui," thought as that on which you rely upon not to disintegrate (A. Tardits).

What part did aesthetic thought play in Joyce's development? At this stage of our inquiry and with due consideration of the twofold nature of the question, the man and the work, the subjective existence and the objective production, it is clear that the answer would require volumes. I shall confine myself to a few observations.

Joyce's brooding on the beautiful and the good, no less than its failure, encouraged a change in his perspective, or, more probably, verified that perspective, as the act of "seeing through" the real, was the thing. The shift in metaphor from "Stephen Hero" to "A Portrait of the Artist as a Young Man" is characteristic and hardly needs developing. Thought ceased to be the crowning glory, the magnum opus. Joyce discovered it to be only the fulcrum on which to rely in order to displace the onus he had carried on guilty shoulders. *Consonantia* could analyze itself, so to speak, into *dissonantia*.[13] The Mystery of the Trinity (the background of Aquinas's contribution to the theory of Beauty as a nodal point in Joyce's theorizing) implied consonance in Love between the persons; but its very existence and persistence in Christian tradition through the ages appeared inseparable from the existence of heretics and from the fight against the Evil they represented.[14] The (Nietzschean) problematics of "genealogy"—that is, how to select the true pretender—tended to be substituted for the dogmas concerning the procession of the persons in the Trinity.

The concept of nature, so central to the *Poetics*, the *Politics*, and the *Nicomachean Ethics* provided another nice set of aporia, when put into historical perspective. How can one account for man's bestiality, bestial appetites? The question recurs again and again in the *Portrait of the Artist*. But it was susceptible of widely different answers. For Aristotle, bestiality falls outside the scope of humanity; for Christian theology, as sin, it raised the question of damnation and redemption, as we have seen; for criminology, biological, psychological, and sociological determinants had to be considered. Taking a different stand altogether, long before Claude Lévi-Strauss, Joyce discovered that man's nature is his symbolic culture: that we meet him in very concrete terms in the context of the "moral history of [a] country." The true nature of man as a political animal (Aristotle's *Politics*), as part and expression of city life, is one essential characteristic of the modern perspective. His legitimate place and status no longer needed to be metaphorized in terms of labyrinth and legendary hero, *sub specie aeternitatis:* the city and the metonymics of its citizens were to be remorselessly affirmed, *sub specie temporis nostri,*[15] as both objects and subject. The model for the 1904 "Portrait of the Artist" pleaded that a "thousand eternities were to be reaffirmed." Things were now going to be different: the reaffirmation was going to be of the Real, though in another connection bound to change its nature. The Eternal's eternity had ceased to obscure man's time.

Nearly ten years after abandoning his "Aesthetic," in his 1912 Padua examination paper, "The Universal Literary Influence of the Renaissance," Joyce affirmed the paradox that "the Renaissance . . . has put the journalist in the monk's chair: that is to say, has deposed an acute, limited and formal mentality to give the sceptre to a mentality that is facile and wide-ranging . . . , a restless and rather amorphous mentality."[16] His analysis sums up his ethical approach to the aesthetic age, as distinct from the Aesthetic movement: "We might say indeed that modern man has an epidermis rather than a soul. The sensory power of his body has developed enormously, but it has developed to the detriment of the spiritual faculty. We lack moral sense and perhaps also strength of imagination."

The description of the physical and psychological condition of the modern subject, which echoes the Lacanian analysis of Joyce's symptom, does ring like a genuine confession. However, Joyce insists on "the untiring creative force, the hot and lively passionate temperament, the intense desire to see and sense" that goes into the making of Renaissance mentality and must be put to its credit: "If the Renaissance did nothing else, it would have done much in creating in ourselves and in our art the sense of compassion for each thing that lives and hopes and dies and deludes itself. In this at least we surpass the ancients: in this the ordinary journalist is greater than the theologian."

The final emphasis is on the love of life, of living, mortal, and erring beings: a new perspective that Joyce was soon going to create and illustrate with Leopold and Molly Bloom. He accepts his lack of imagination because there also lies the way to the "literary" compensation that the epiphanies, as "trivial" encounters duly sublimized, formulated and promoted. After all, his move from aesthetics to ethics was already implicit in his fascination with Augustine's observation: "It was manifested unto me that those things be good which yet are corrupted; which neither if they were supremely good, nor unless they were good could be corrupted: for had they been supremely good they would have been incorruptible but if they were not good there would be nothing in them which could be corrupted."[17]

When Joyce listed "Problems" for his "Aesthetic," he gave them complete with answers: the matter to be established was the abstract nature of the "work of art." But other questions in his 1903–4 Notebook (Appendix B) are not answered. The same is true in the *Portrait of the Artist*, in which they are deliberately presented as his starting point:

> I have a book at home . . . in which I have written down questions. . . . In finding the answers to them I found the theory of esthetic which I am trying to explain. Here are some questions I set myself: *Is a chair finely made tragic or comic? Is the portrait of Mona Lisa good if I desire to see it? Is the bust of Sir Philip Crampton lyrical, epical or dramatic? If not, why not? . . . If a man hacking in fury at a block of wood . . . make there an image of a cow, is that image a work of art? If not, why not?* (PA, 214)

The reason why they are not answered is clear: they bear on the nature of the beautiful and the good, on the relationship of author and reader or spectator, on the symbolism of colors, on positive or negative desire. In short, questions involving subjectivity appear insoluble, absurd, beyond the confines of conscious reasoning. Theory was failing him when it came to answering these aporia, to finding the letters answering the *aloga* of experience, the improbable things beyond reasonable discourse which were, however, proper material for the poet, as Aristotle maintained in the *Poetics*. It is quite probable that Joyce envisaged such questions on the model of the Aquinan *quaestio disputata*, the starting point of doctrinal exposition. But they turned out to be *problema*, in more than one sense.

Once more, *Stephen Hero* offers interesting confirmation of Joyce's strategy as Stephen: "He gave himself no great trouble to sustain to boldnesses which were expressed or implied in his essays. He threw them out as sudden defence-works while he was busy constructing the enigma of a manner. For the youth had been apprised of another crisis and he wished to make ready for the shock of it" (*SH*, 27). Joyce indeed *needed* to confront nonsense, the absurd, the irrational, not so much to defend himself against the others, rather to defend himself against himself. He was not "dressing up the character," assuming a pose. He was building up an ego from the inside, from the point of view of an *evasive enunciation*, enigma answering crisis.

Problema, according to Liddell and Scott's *Greek-English Lexicon*, means: 1) anything thrown or projected forward, obstacle; 2) defence, bulwark; 3) anything put forward as an excuse; and 4) task. Joyce's itinerary was from task[18] through excuse and defense back to obstacle and ultimately to what is thrown before you, the daily trivia, the triviality that is the proper subject matter of daily papers; and he was careful not to leave anything en route in the way of excuse, and so forth. The starting point was the epiphanic problem, analyzed in terms of letters.[19] His genius, which may be after all that of his age as well as his own, was to realize that this symptomatic encounter had been of the Voice and the Letter. The epiphany proposed in *Stephen Hero* tells of the real, paradigmatic encounter: it tells of *what may be missed*, of possible failure without, however, affirming success. The encounter so defined (but isn't it its very definition?) is of boy and girl, of law and transgression, and, ultimately, when it comes to writing out the problem thus set, of what cannot be heard ("inaudibly") and what cannot be written: (". . ."), (". . ."): the Name of the Father and the Book, only from an angle that questions their certitude while asserting their permanence for and in the writing subject.

I have minimized influences and knowledge, the possible individual influences of those who, at one point or another, Joyce thought to have "known better." I felt that the considerable scholarship that Joyce had amassed and put into his thinking only convinced him that he had been answering the wrong calls. "His errors were the portals of discovery": error, (self-) betrayal, lapses, and other dissonances had only to be affirmed.

It took Joyce some time, and a few pages, to realize that he really belonged to the *post*-Hegelian moment, in a sense to the Nietzschean moment, when "the legitimacy of man's viewpoint was reaffirmed against the Divine," asserting "the real as multiplicity, fragmentation, difference, that only art can adequately grasp."[20] Epiphanies did not belong to the world of facts and could not be "comprehended," in Joyce's words, by science. Neither were they manifestations of truth, for truth was no longer of the order of revelation. It was to be approached in terms of scriptural production, as modern historiography was to demonstrate.[21] Joyce's art, writing[22] was sustained in its development by contemporary analyses of language more or less directly derived from philology, and by modern theories of interpretation that renewed and enriched the long tradition initiated by Aristotle. The letter was gradually reaffirmed as indispensable to the spirit, and the only way of sustaining life in both artist and artwork,[23] his scriptural errors leading him from one *écriture* to another, each providing him with temporary *appui*. Reading about the problems set by philosophers and religious thinkers, confronting them with his own, reading through other writers' (Mangan, Leopardi, Ibsen, etc.) difficulties, crises, far from leading him to atonement and reconciliation with a *lex eterna*, helped lead him to an acceptance of his own contradictions and necessities, duly refined into his own ineluctable Necessity: his writing as scriptural act making History.

Aristotle: The Paris Sources

·

APPENDIX B demonstrates that Joyce's main source was J. Barthélémy-Saint-Hilaire's translation of Aristotle's *Oeuvres*. But Joyce also consulted the *Metaphysics* in Victor Cousin's selection, a volume that deserves special attention.[1] The full title is *De la Métaphysique d'Aristotle: Rapport sur le concours ouvert par l'Académie des Sciences Morales et Politiques, suivi d'un essai de traduction du premier et du douzième livres de la "Métaphysique."*[2] So not only is the volume a partial translation of the treatise, it is basically a report on the dissertations submitted to the Académie in 1833, the subject being: "1) to give an account of the book [Aristotle's *Metaphysics*] through a full analysis and general outline; 2) to write its history and point out its influence on later systems in modern as well as ancient times; 3) to discern and discuss errors and truths therein, which of its notions have survived to the present day, especially those which might be of practical value to contemporary philosophy."[3]

In short, Cousin's book was in harmony with Joyce's (and Bosanquet's and Butcher's for that matter) desire to conciliate modern and ancient philosophy. Its most interesting portion is the report on the dissertation that eventually won the prize, that of Felix Ravaisson, who, even before his celebrated thesis on *L'Habitude* (1838), was to expand it into an *Essai sur la Métaphysique d'Aristotle* (1837). Here is Cousin's summary of Ravaisson's argument:

The author tries to demonstrate that matter in peripatetic metaphysics plays approximately the same role as the Idea in Platonic doctrine. Now matter exists only through the determination imposed upon it, just as form does not exist outside matter. Peripatetic form is precisely the individual element in thing. In logic it is differentia; and just as in the outside world form is what constitutes reality, so in logic differentia, not genre, is the essential characteristic of a definition. *Essence therefore lies in difference,* in individuality. Matter is then a mere possibility of being; form is what realizes that possibility and give actuality: *form is an energy* . . . it is the active element. (Italics mine)[4]

That difference is of the essence was certainly a statement that Joyce could not only subscribe to but also welcome as a landmark in his own theoretical investigations. And Ravaisson's conclusions on matter as the possible and form as energy was food certainly for Stephen's—and most probably for Joyce's—thoughts.

It is worth observing, however, that this stay in Paris may have been the occasion for Joyce to read other books equally relevant to his inquiry into "the living doctrine of the *Poetics*."[5] One of them is indeed a scholarly edition of the *Poetics,* the most recent then in France, whose editors were drawing attention to the necessity of relating that treatise to other works of the Stagyrite, which are proved to have enlisted Joyce's attention then: as the Introduction points out, after due acknowledgements to Ravaisson, "all the parts of that vast whole [Aristotle's system] can be judged only with consideration of their close mutual relationships and of the doctrine which holds them tightly knit together."[6] The editors do insist on referring the reader to the *Rhetoric,* the *Nichomachean Ethics,* and so forth; they also devote a great part of their Introduction to a reconstruction of the Aristotelian theory of comedy, another topic fully consonant with Joyce's preoccupations.

Another book that may have then given Joyce some mental sustenance is Ernest Renan's doctoral dissertation, *Averroës et l'averroïsme,*[7] which he was to praise a few years later in "Ireland, Island of Saints and Sages."[8] The book, which, by the way, contains a number of references to Ravaisson's study, provides a full discussion and an original theory of intellect (active and passive) based on the first and third books of the *De anima* and book 12 of the *Metaphysics*, which Joyce was then studying. Averroës's conciliation of theology and philosophy was to have lasting effects on Western culture, putting Aquinas in the paradoxical position of being, in Renan's words, "both the most serious adversary the Averroist doctrine ever met and . . . the first disciple of 'the Great Commentator. . . . As a philosopher, Saint Thomas Aquinas owes almost everything to Averroes." In *Ulysses* Stephen Dedalus muses: "Gone too from the world, Averroes and Moses Maimonides, dark men in mien and movement, flashing in their mocking mirrors the obscure soul of the world, a darkness shining in brightness which brightness could not comprehend."[9] That Joyce became acquainted with Averroës's doctrine in Paris may be conjectured from the context: only a couple of pages earlier, explicit allusion is made to such an episode in the protagonist's personal history:

> It must be a movement then, an actuality of the possible as possible. Aristotle's phrase formed itself within the gabbled verses and floated out into the studious silence of the library of Sainte-Geneviève where he had read, sheltered from the sin of Paris, night by night. By his elbow a delicate Siamese conned a handbook of strategy. Fed and feeding brains about me: under glowlamps, impaled, with faintly beating feelers: and in my mind's darkness a sloth of the underworld, reluctant, shy of brightness, shifting her dragon's scaly folds. Thought is the thought of thought. Tranquil brightness. The soul is in a manner all that is: the soul is the form of forms. Tranquillity sudden, vast, candescent: form of forms.[10]

The line of descent from Aristotle to Joyce through Averroës and Aquinas, substantially valid, points to a projected conciliation of theology with philosophy which may be observed also in the broader fields of Renaissance and seventeenth-century philosophy and ideology.

The detail of Joyce's notes in Appendix B demonstrates that Aristotle could also appear to him as paving the way toward modern theories of interpretation centering on psychology and extending into logic, ethics, and metaphysics. These notes, then, should not blind us to the fact that they are part of Joyce's more general interest in interpretative reading and the interpretative tradition. We have already met Dante and the Neoplatonic. Joyce quite early presented Vico as pre-Freudian.[11] But it may also be argued that Joyce owed something to Marx, who is one of the "subversive writers" in whose company Stephen Dedalus is supposed to waste his youth (*PA*, 78) and who inspired the closing lines of "A Portrait of the Artist" (1904): for he also spoke of the limits of human experience, of the "laws not only independent of human will, consciousness and intelligence, but rather, on the contrary, determining that will, consciousness and intelligence."[12]

Taking a still broader view, it may be observed that Joyce's effort at theorizing the epiphanic experience in terms of (Aristotle's) psychology *and* science parallels the philosophical development from Franz Brentano, another great commentator of the *De anima,* to Husserl. For Husserl, modern phenomenoloy indicates the moment when philosophy leaves the prescientific age and acquires a status as a science, just as Joyce's aesthetic, from the same starting point, aims at establishing the basis for a modern science of letters. No wonder then that the Irish writer was to have such an appeal for, or impact on, contemporary thinkers, especially Lacan and Derrida.

Quotations from Aristotle in Joyce's 1903–1904 Notebooks

.

The soul is the first entelechy of a naturally organic body.

SOURCE: *Psychologie d'Aristote. Traité de l'âme,* traduit en français pour la première fois, et accompagné de notes perpétuelles, par J. Barthélémy-Saint-Hilaire (Paris, Librairie Philosophique Ladrange, 1846, p. 165): "L'âme est l'entéléchie première d'un corps naturel organique."

ENGLISH TRANSLATION: Aristotle *On the Soul* II.i.412a27 (Loeb Classical Library, p. 69): "The soul may . . . be defined as the first actuality of a natural body potentially possessing life; and such will be any body which possesses organs."

The most natural act for living beings which are complete is to produce other beings like themselves and thereby to participate as far as they may in the eternal and divine.

SOURCE: Ibid., pp. 187–88: "L'acte le plus naturel aux êtres vivants qui sont complets, et qui ne sont ni avortés, ni produits par génération spontanée, c'est de produire un autre être pareil à eux, l'animal un animal, la plante une plante, afin de participer de l'éternel et du divin autant qu'ils le peuvent."

ENGLISH TRANSLATION: Ibid. II.iv.415a26 (Loeb Classical Library, pp. 85–86): "This is the most natural of all functions among living creatures, provided that they are perfect and not maimed, and do not have spontaneous generation: *viz.,* to reproduce one's kind, an animal producing an animal, and a plant a plant, in order that they may have a share in the immortal and divine in the only way they can."

A voice is a sound which expresses something.

SOURCE: Ibid., p. 226: "La voix est un son exprimant quelque chose."

ENGLISH TRANSLATION: Ibid. II.viii.420b33 (Loeb Classical Library, p. 119): "The voice is a sound which means something."

In the sense of touch man is far above all other animals and hence he is the most intelligent animal.

SOURCE: Ibid, p. 228: "Mais pour le toucher, il est fort au-dessus d'eux tous, ce qui fait aussi qu'il est le plus intelligent des animaux."

ENGLISH TRANSLATION: Ibid. II.ix.421a21 (Loeb Classical Library, p. 121): "In the other senses he is behind many kinds of animals, but in touch he is much more discriminating than the other animals. This is why he is of all living creatures the most intelligent."

Men who have tough flesh have not much intelligence.

SOURCE: Ibid., p. 229: "Les hommes qui ont la chair dure sont mal doués pour l'intelligence."

ENGLISH TRANSLATION: Ibid.: "Men of hard skin and flesh are poorly, and men of soft flesh well endowed with intelligence."

The flesh is the intermediary for the sense of touch.

SOURCE: Ibid., p. 245: "C'est la chair qui est l'intermédiaire pour l'organe qui touche."

ENGLISH TRANSLATION: Ibid. II.xi.423b17 (Loeb Classical Library, p. 133): "As air and water are related to vision, hearing and smell, so is the relation of the flesh and the tongue to the sense organ in the case of touch."

A sense receives the form without the matter.

SOURCE: Ibid., p. 247: "Le sens est ce qui reçoit les formes sensibles sans la matière."

ENGLISH TRANSLATION: Ibid. II.xii.424a18 (Loeb Classical Library, p. 137): "Sense is that which is receptive of the form of sensible objects without the matter."

The sensation of particular things is always true.

SOURCE: Ibid., p. 278: "La sensation des choses particulières est toujours vraie."

ENGLISH TRANSLATION: Ibid. III.iii.428b18 (Loeb Classical Library, p. 163): "The perception of proper objects is true, or is only capable of error to the least possible degree."

That which acts is superior to that which suffers.

SOURCE: Ibid., p. 303: "Ce qui agit est supérieur à ce qui souffre."

ENGLISH TRANSLATION: Ibid. III.v.430a18 (Loeb Classical Library, p. 171): "The agent is always superior to the patient."

Only when it is separate from all things is the intellect really itself and this intellect separate from all things is immortal and divine.

SOURCE: Ibid., p. 304: "C'est seulement quand elle est séparée que l'intelligence est vraiment ce qu'elle est; et cette intelligence seule est immortelle et éternelle."

ENGLISH TRANSLATION: Ibid. III.v.430a22 (Loeb Classical Library, p. 171): "When isolated [mind] is its true self and nothing more, and this alone is immortal and everlasting."

Error is not found apart from combination.

SOURCE: Ibid., p. 307: "C'est que l'erreur, ici non plus, ne se trouve jamais que dans la combinaison."

ENGLISH TRANSLATION: Ibid. III.vi.430b2 (Loeb Classical Library, p. 173): "Falsehood always lies in the process of combination."

The principle which hates is not different from the principle which loves.

SOURCE: Ibid., p. 315: "Le principe qui, dans l'âme, désire, et celui qui hait, ne sont pas différents entre aux."

ENGLISH TRANSLATION: Ibid. III.vii.431a13 (Loeb Classical Library, pp. 175–76): "The faculties of appetite or avoidance are not really different from each other."

The intellect conceives the forms of the images presented to it.

SOURCE: Ibid., pp. 317–18: "L'âme intelligente pense les formes dans les images qu'elle perçoit."

ENGLISH TRANSLATION: Ibid. III.vii.431b2 (Loeb Classical Library, p. 177): "The thinking faculty thinks the forms in mental images."

The intellectual soul is the form of forms.[1]

SOURCE: Ibid., p. 322: "L'intelligence est la forme des formes."

ENGLISH TRANSLATION: Ibid. III.viii.432a2 (Loeb Classical Library, p. 181): "The mind is a form which employs forms."

The soul is in a manner all that is.[2]

SOURCE: Ibid., p. 320: "L'âme est en somme tout ce qui est."

ENGLISH TRANSLATION: Ibid. III.viii.431b21 (Loeb Classical Library, p. 179): "In a sense the soul is of all existing things."

Color is the limit of the diaphane in any determined body.[3]

SOURCE: *Psychologie d'Aristote, Opuscules (Parva Naturalia)*, translated by J. Barthélémy-Saint-Hilaire, Paris, Dumont, 1847, "De la sensation et des choses sensibles," p. 40: "La couleur est la limite du diaphane dans un corps déterminé."

ENGLISH TRANSLATION: Aristotle, *On Sense and Sensible Objects* III.439bII (Loeb Classical Library, p. 231): "Since color resides in the limit, it must lie in the limit of the transparent. Hence color will be the limit of the transparent in a defined body."

Nature always acts in the view of some end.

SOURCE: Ibid., "Du sommeil," p. 140: "La nature fait toujours toutes choses en vue de quelque fin."

ENGLISH TRANSLATION: Aristotle, *On Sleep and Waking*, II.455b17 (Loeb Classical Library, p. 331): "We hold that nature acts with some end in view."

The end of every being is its greatest good.

SOURCE: Ibid., "Du sommeil et de la veille," p. 157: "Sentir et penser est la fin véritable de tous les êtres qui ont l'une ou l'autre de ces facultés, parce qu'elles sont leur plus grand bien et que la fin de chaque être est toujours son bien le plus grand."

ENGLISH TRANSLATION: Ibid. II.455b25 (Loeb Classical Library, p. 331): "Perception or thinking is the proper end of all creatures which have either of these capacities, since they represent what is best, and the end is what is best."

Speculation is above practice.

SOURCE: *Métaphysique d'Aristote,* translated by J. Barthélémy-Saint-Hilaire,

Paris, Germer-Baillère, 1879, p. 12: "L'homme qui se guide par les données de l'art est supérieur à ceux qui suivent exclusivement l'expérience; l'architecte au-dessus des manoeuvres; et les sciences de théorie sont au-dessus des sciences purement pratiques."

ENGLISH TRANSLATION: Aristotle, *Metaphysics* I.i.982a1 (Loeb Classical Library, p. 9): "The man of experience is held to be wiser than the mere possessor of any power of sensation, the artist than the man of experience, the master craftsman than the artisan; and the speculative sciences to be more learned than the productive."

The wood does not make the bed nor the bronze the statue.

SOURCE: Ibid., p. 33: "Le bois ne fait pas le lit, ni le bronze la statue."

ENGLISH TRANSLATION: Ibid. I.iii.984a24–25 (Loeb Classical Library, p. 23): "Wood does not make a bed, nor bronze a statue."

One who has only opinion is, compared with one who knows, in a state of sickness with regard to truth.

SOURCE: Ibid., p. 49: "Comparativement à l'homme qui sait les choses, celui qui ne s'en forme qu'une vague opinion n'est pas dans une santé parfaite par rapport à la vérité."

ENGLISH TRANSLATION: Ibid. IV.iv.1008b30–31 (Loeb Classical Library, p. 181): "Indeed the man who guesses, as contrasted with him who knows, is not in a healthy relation to the truth."

The same attribute cannot at the same time and in the same connection belong and not belong to the same subject.[4]

SOURCE: Ibid., p. 25: "Il est impossible qu'une seule et même chose soit, et tout à la fois ne soit pas, à une même autre chose, sous un même rapport."

ENGLISH TRANSLATION: Ibid. IV.iii.1005b20 (Loeb Classical Library, p. 161): "It is impossible for the same attribute at once to belong and not to belong to the same thing and in the same relation."

There cannot be a middle term between two contrary propositions.

SOURCE: Ibid., p. 73: "Il ne peut y avoir de moyen terme entre deux propositions contraires."

ENGLISH TRANSLATION: Ibid. IV.vii.1011b24–25 (Loeb Classical Library, p. 199): "Nor indeed can there be any intermediate between contrary statements."

Necessity is that in virtue of which it is impossible that a thing should be otherwise.

SOURCE: Ibid., p. 109: "Quand une chose ne peut pas être autrement qu'elle n'est, nous déclarons qu'il est nécessaire qu'elle soit ce qu'elle est."

ENGLISH TRANSLATION: Ibid. V.v.1015a34–35 (Loeb Classical Library, p. 225): "What cannot be otherwise we say is necessarily so."

The hand is not (absolutely) part of the body.[5]

SOURCE: Ibid., p. 327: "La main, absolument parlant, n'est pas une partie de l'homme; elle est uniquement la main en tant qu'elle est animée."

ENGLISH TRANSLATION: Ibid. VII.xi.1036b30 (Loeb Classical Library, p. 367): "It is not the hand in *any* condition that is a part of a man, but only when it can perform its function, and so has life in it."

It is in beings that are always the same and are not susceptible of change that we must seek for [the] truth.

SOURCE: Ibid., p. 101: "On ne doit chercher à trouver la vérité que dans les choses qui sont éternellement les mêmes, et qui ne subissent jamais le moindre changement."

ENGLISH TRANSLATION: Ibid. XI.vi.1063a13 (Loeb Classical Library, p. 79): "It is by reference to those things which are always in the same state and undergo no change that we should prosecute our search for truth." Aristotle continues: "Of this kind are the heavenly bodies; for these do not appear to be now of one nature and subsequently of another, but are manifestly always the same and have no more part in change of any kind" [See Jacques Lacan, *Le Séminaire, Livre VII, L'Ethique de la psychanalyse*, 91].

Movement is the actuality of the possible as possible.[6]

SOURCE: *Physique*, translated by J. Barthélémy-Saint-Hilaire, Paris, p. 85: "Le mouvement peut être défini très convenablement: l'acte ou entéléchie du possible en tant que possible."

ENGLISH TRANSLATION: *Aristotle's Physics*, translated by Hippocrates Apostle, Indiana University Press, Bloomington, 1969, III.i.200.10–11: "A motion is [defined as] the actuality of the potentially existing qua existing potentially."

Thought is the thought of thought.

SOURCE: *Métaphysique d'Aristote*, translated by Victor Cousin, Paris, Ladrange, 1838, XII.vii: "La pensée est la pensée de la pensée."

ENGLISH TRANSLATION: Ibid. XII.vii.1072b20 (Loeb Classical Library, p. 149): "Thought thinks itself through participation in the object of thought."

God is the eternal perfect animal.

SOURCE: Ibid. XII.vii: "Dieu est un animal éternel et parfait."

ENGLISH TRANSLATION: Ibid. XII.vii.1072b29 (Loeb Classical Library, p. 151): "God is a living being, eternal, most good."

(The object of desire is that which appears to us *beautiful*. . . . We desire a thing because it appears to us *good*. . . (?) *Met*. XII cap.7.)

SOURCE: *Métaphysique d'Aristote,* translated by J. Barthélémy-Saint-Hilaire, p. 181: "L'objet désiré est ce qui nous paraît être bien; . . . nous souhaitons [le bien] parce qu'il nous paraît souhaitable, bien plutôt qu'il ne nous paraît souhaitable parce que nous le souhaitons."

ENGLISH TRANSLATION: Ibid. XII.vii.1072a29 (Loeb Classical Library, p. 147): "The primary objects of desire and thought are the same. For it is the apparent good that is the object of appetite, and the real good that is the object of the rational will. Desire is the result of opinion rather than opinion that of desire."

Nature, it seems, is not a collection of unconnected episodes, like a tragedy ["bad dream (or drama)" in Herbert Gorman's biography of Joyce].

SOURCE: Ibid. t. 3, p. 335: "D'après tout ce que nous voyons, la nature ne montre pas à nos yeux une succession de vains épisodes, comme one en trouve dans une mauvaise tragédie."

ENGLISH TRANSLATION: Ibid. XIV.iii.1090b19–20 (Loeb Classical Library, p. 281): "It does not appear, to judge from the observed facts, that the natural system lacks cohesion, like a poorly constructed drama.

.

From Joyce's 1903–1904 Notebooks: Questions

1. I desire to see the Mona Lisa. Is it therefore beautiful or is it good?
2. Spicer-Simson has made a bust of his wife. Is it lyrical, epical, or dramatic?
3. Is a chair finely made tragic or comic?
4. Why are statues made white for the most part?

The Pola Notebook

·

Bonum est in quod tendit appetitus. S. Thomas Aquinas.

The good is that towards the possession of which an appetite tends: the good is the desirable. The true and the beautiful are the most persistent orders of the desirable. Truth is desired by the intellectual appetite which is appeased by the most satisfying relations of the intelligible; beauty is desired by the aesthetic appetite which is appeased by the most satisfying relations of the sensible. The true and the beautiful are spiritually possessed; the true by intellection, the beautiful by apprehension, and the appetites which desire to possess them, the intellectual and aesthetic appetites, are therefore spiritual appetites . . .

J. A. J. Pola, 7 XI 04

Pulchra sunt quae visa placent. S. Thomas Aquinas.

Those things are beautiful the apprehension of which pleases. Therefore beauty is that quality of a sensible object in virtue of which its apprehension pleases or satisfies the aesthetic appetite which desires to apprehend the most satisfying relations of the sensible. Now the act of apprehension involves at least two activities, the activity of cognition or simple perception and the activity of recognition. If the activity of simple perception is, like every other activity, itself pleasant, every sensible object that has been apprehended can be said in the first place to have been and to be in a measure beautiful; and even the most hideous object can be said to have been and to be beautiful in so far as it has been apprehended. In regard then to that part of the act of apprehension which is called the activity of simple perception there is no sensible object which cannot be said to be in a measure beautiful.

With regard to the second part of the act of apprehension which is called the activity of recognition it may further be said that there is no activity of simple perception to which there does not succeed in whatsoever measure the activity of recognition. For by the activity of recognition is meant an activity of decision; and in accordance with this activity in all conceivable cases a sensible object is said to be satisfying or dissatisfying. But the activity of recognition is, like every other activity, itself pleasant and therefore every object that has been apprehended is secondly in whatsoever measure beautiful. Consequently even the most hideous object may be said to be beautiful for this reason as it is a priori said to be beautiful in so far as it encounters the activity of simple perception.

Sensible objects, however, are said conventionally to be beautiful or not for neither of the foregoing reasons but rather by reason of the nature, degree and duration of the satisfaction resulting from the apprehension of them and it is in accordance with these latter merely that the words "beautiful" and "ugly" are used in practical aesthetic philosophy. It remains then to be said that these words indicate only a greater or less measure of resultant satisfaction and that any sensible object, to which the word "ugly" is practically applied, an object, that is, the apprehension of which results in a small measure of aesthetic satisfaction, is, in so far as its apprehension results in any measure of satisfaction whatsoever, said to be for the third time beautiful . . .

J. A. J. Pola, 15 XI 04

APPENDIX C

The Act of Apprehension

It has been said that the act of apprehension involves at least two activities—the activity of cognition or simple perception and the activity of recognition. The act of apprehension, however, in its most complete form involves three activities—the third being the activity of satisfaction. By reason of the fact that these three activities are all pleasant themselves every sensible object that has been apprehended must be doubly and may be trebly beautiful. In practical aesthetic philosophy the epithets "beautiful" and "ugly" are applied with regard chiefly to the third activity, with regard, that is, to the nature, degree and duration of the satisfaction resultant from the apprehension of any sensible object and therefore any sensible object to which in practical aesthetic philosophy the epithet "beautiful" is applied must be trebly beautiful, must have encountered, that is, the three activities which are involved in the act of apprehension in its most complete form. Practically then the quality of beauty in itself must involve three constituents to encounter each of these three activities . . .

J. A. J. Pola. 16 XI 04

NOTES

·

Prolegomena

1. See Richard Ellmann, *James Joyce* (1959; rev. ed., London: Oxford University Press, 1982), passim.
2. *Freeman's Journal*, 1 June 1907. Quoted in *Workshop*, 164.
3. *Workshop*, 147. See also Constantine Curran, *James Joyce Remembered* (London: Oxford University Press, 1968).
4. Ellmann, *James Joyce*, 119.
5. *CW*, 84–140.
6. Herbert Gorman, *James Joyce* (New York: Reinhart, 1940), chap. 5.
7. Ellmann, *James Joyce*, part 2.
8. *Letters*, 2:38.
9. *The Complete Dublin Diary of Stanislaus Joyce*, ed. George H. Healey (Ithaca: Cornell University Press, 1971), 2.
10. The manuscript intended by W. B. Yeats as a Preface to *Ideas of Good and Evil* (1903), in Richard Ellmann, *The Identity of Yeats* (New York: Oxford University Press, 1954), 86–89. The interview in question took place in fall 1902.
11. *The Complete Dublin Diary of Stanislaus Joyce*, 53n.
12. See also *PA*, 176, for a reference to Stephen's "search for the essence of beauty amid the spectral words of Aristotle or Aquinas."
13. William T. Noon, *Joyce and Aquinas: A Study of the Religious Elements in the Writing of James Joyce* (New Haven: Yale University Press; London: Oxford University Press, 1957).
14. Jean Jacquot, "L'Esthétique de Joyce," in *Mélanges Georges Jamati* (Editions du C.N.R.S., 1956), 143.
15. Etienne Gilson, *Matières et formes* (Paris: Librairie Philosophique Vrin, 1964), 16.
16. Ibid., 10–11.

17. Ibid., 17.
18. *Workshop*, 150.
19. Gorman, *James Joyce*, 94.
20. *Workshop*, 67.
21. Anthony Ward, *Walter Pater: The Idea in Nature* (London: MacGibbon & Kee, 1966), 44. See also Madeleine L. Cazamian, *L'Anti-intellectualisme et l'Esthétisme, 1880–1900*, vol. 2 of *Le Roman et les idées en Angleterre*, 3rd ed. (Paris: Les Belles-Lettres, 1935), 16.
22. G. W. F. Hegel, *Aesthetic*, trans. William M. Bryant (New York: Appleton & Co., 1879), part 2.
23. G. W. F. Hegel and C. L. Michelet, *The Philosophy of Art: An Introduction to the Scientific Study of Aesthetics*, trans. from the German by William Hastie (Edinburgh: Oliver & Boyd, 1886). A French translation had also been available since the mid-nineteenth century: G. W. F. Hegel, *Cours d'esthétique*, trans. Charles Magloire Bénard, 5 vols. (Paris and Nancy, 1840–52), which Joyce had the opportunity, though hardly enough time, to study in Paris in 1902–3.
24. G. W. F. Hegel, *The Introduction to Hegel's "Philosophy of Fine Art,"* translated from the German, with notes and prefatory essay, by Bernard Bosanquet (London: Kegan Paul, Trench, Trübner & Co., 1886).
25. Bosanquet.
26. See, for example, the opening statements in chap. 1 below.
27. Butcher.
28. See Butcher's Preface to the 1895 edition of ibid.
29. Butcher's Preface to the 1897 edition of ibid., xx: "I desire to acknowledge my obligation to friends, such as Mr B. Bosanquet (whose *History of Aesthetic* ought to be in the hands of all students of the subject)."
30. Butcher, 1895 edition, 108.
31. Bosanquet, 468.

CHAPTER ONE
Explorations

1. *CW,* 17–30.
2. The editors of the *Critical Writings* point out that "Stanislaus Joyce used the back of the sheets for his diary, so preserving

'Force' (the first essay) and the three essays that follow it ('The Study of Languages,' 'Royal Irish Academy "Ecce Homo,"' 'Drama and Life')."

3. *CW,* 17–24. The essay is dated "27-9-98."

4. Richard Ellmann, *James Joyce* (1959; rev. ed., London: Oxford University Press, 1982), 68. We shall soon have a confirmation of such an influence.

5. Anthony Ward, *Walter Pater: The Idea in Nature* (London: MacGibbon & Kee, 1966), 67.

6. Walter Pater, *Appreciations, with an Essay on Style,* vol. 1 of *Works,* 10 vols. (1899; Library Edition, London: Macmillan, 1910), 1:62 and 81–82.

7. William Wallace, *Prolegomena to the Study of Hegel's Philosophy and Especially of His Logic,* 2d ed. (Oxford, 1894), 157. Quoted in Ward, *Walter Pater: The Idea in Nature,* 69.

8. G. W. F. Hegel, *Esthétique,* 3rd ed., 4 vols. (Paris: Aubier, 1944), 2:156–57 (translation mine).

9. See F. S. L. Lyons, *Ireland since the Famine* (1971; rev. ed., London: Weidenfeld & Nicholson, 1973), part 2, chap. 5, "The Battle of Two Civilisations."

10. Ellmann, *James Joyce,* 61. See also Joyce's letter to Stanislaus, 6 November 1906, in *Letters,* 2:187: "If the Irish programme did not insist on the Irish language, I suppose I could call myself a nationalist."

11. *The Works of John Ruskin,* ed. E. T. Cook and Alexander Wedderburn, Library Edition, 39 vols. (London: George Allen, 1903–12), 23:379.

12. Ibid., 382–408.

13. *U,* 21, 208 (Sabellius); 21, 38, 523 (Arius); 28, 390 (Averroës).

14. See Frances A. Yates, *The Art of Memory* (London: Routledge & Kegan Paul, 1966).

15. Aristotle, *Metaphysics* 1078a, in Bosanquet, 33.

16. Bosanquet, 33, quoting *Philebus,* marg. 64.

17. See Hugh Kenner, "Joyce and the Nineteenth-Century Linguistic Explosion," in *Atti del Third International James Joyce Symposium* (Trieste: Università degli Studi, Facoltà di Magistero, 1974); and Richard Chenevix Trench, *On the Study of Words* (London: John W. Parker & Son, 1851), chap. 3.

18. Bosanquet, chap. 7.

19. First published in 1890. Quotations are from *Oeuvres complètes* (Paris: Calmann-Lévy, 1947–61), vol. 3 (translation mine).

20. Michel Foucault, *The Order of Things* (London: Tavistock Publications, 1970), 299–300.
21. *The Complete Dublin Diary of Stanislaus Joyce,* ed. George H. Healey (Ithaca: Cornell University Press, 1971), 53. See also 2.
22. The editors of the *Critical Writings* suggest that Joyce had in mind such statements of Leonardo as this one from the *Notebooks* (McCurdy ed., 2:261): "You may readily deceive yourself by selecting such faces as bear a resemblance to your own, since it would often seem that such similarities please us; and if you were ugly you would not select beautiful faces, but would be creating ugly faces like many faces whose types often resemble their master."

CHAPTER TWO

The Dramatic Idea and Beyond

1. See Charles Andler, *Nietzsche,* 3 vols. (Paris: Gallimard, 1958), 1:371–99.
2. See Jean Noel, *George Moore, l'homme et l'oeuvre* (Paris: Marcel Didier, 1966), 291.
3. See, for example, in the *Athenaeum* of 7 November 1896 the preposterous reviews of *Also Sprach Zarathustra, The Case of Wagner, Nietzsche contra Wagner, The Twilight of the Idols,* and *The Anti-Christ.* And in the 1 June 1898 issue Beatrice Marshall insisted on defending Wagner against Nietzsche.
4. As, for example, in his Preface to *Also Sprach Zarathustra.* See also David S. Thatcher, *Nietzsche in England, 1890–1914: The Growth of a Reputation* (Toronto: University of Toronto Press, 1970).
5. Joyce himself was not immune against this oversimplification: see *Letters,* 1:56, in which he signs "Jim Overman."
6. For the ideological stature and impact of the book, see Madeleine L. Cazamian, *Le Roman et les idées en Angleterre,* 3rd ed. (Paris: Les Belles-Lettres, 1935), 2.
7. In April, July, and August 1896.
8. Thatcher, *Nietzsche in England,* 29, 33, and 39.
9. See Herbert Howarth, *The Irish Writers* (New York: Hill & Wang, 1958), 57; and Noel, *George Moore, l'homme et l'oeuvre,* passim.
10. Howarth, *The Irish Writers,* 26.
11. See below, "The Day of the Rabblement."

12. In "The Study of Languages," in *CW,* 28. See also *SH,* 186 and 204.

13. Emile Zola, *Le Roman expérimental* (Paris, 1880); and Claude Bernard, *Introduction à l'étude de la médecine expérimentale* (Paris, 1865). See also Emile Zola's Preface to *Thérèse Raquin:* "J'ai simplement fait sur deux corps vivants le travail analytique que les chirurgiens font sur des cadavres."

14. Estell M. Hurll, *The Madonna in Art* (London: David Nutt, 1899).

15. *Encyclopaedia Britannica,* s.v. "Cartesianism." See also *SH,* 186 and 204, in which the "modern" method is explicitly presented as "vivisective."

16. G. W. F. Hegel, *Esthétique,* 3rd ed., 4 vols. (Paris: Aubier, 1944), 3:212ff. (translation mine).

17. Quoted by Gaëtan Picon in *Encyclopédie de la Littérature française* (Paris: Gallimard, Bibliothèque de la Pléiade), 1132: "A côté du dialogue indispensable, il y a presque toujours un autre dialogue qui semble superflu. . . . C'est le seul que l'âme écoute profondément. . . . Ce que je dis compte souvent pour peu de chose; mais ma présence, l'attitude de mon âme . . . voilà ce qui vous parle en cet instant tragique."

18. Richard Wagner, letter to M. Frédéric Villot, in *The Music of the Future* (London: Schott & Co., 1873), 48.

19. Françoise Frontisi-Ducroux, *Dédale: Mythologie de l'artisan en Grèce ancienne* (Paris: Maspéro, 1975), 98.

20. See Hegel, *Esthétique,* 1:240 and 3:140–41.

21. This is another distinct evocation of Wagner: C. L. Michelet was writing in the last decades of the century, not in the time of Hegel.

22. As spelt out by G. W. F. Hegel and C. L. Michelet, *The Philosophy of Art: An Introduction to the Scientific Study of Aesthetics,* trans. from the German by William Hastie (Edinburgh: Oliver & Boyd, 1886), 100–101.

23. Bosanquet, 484.

24. *Workshop,* 60.

25. Richard Ellmann, *James Joyce* (1959; rev. ed., London: Oxford University Press, 1982), 274.

26. Compare "The Day of the Rabblement," in *CW,* 69: "The artist, though he may employ the crowd, is very careful to isolate himself." And note Wilde's allusion to Renan.

27. Oscar Wilde, *Intentions: The Soul of Man under Socialism* (London: Methuen & Co., 1908), 273 and 292.

28. *Workshop,* 66.
29. Ibid., 72, 75–77, and 101 (Trieste Notebook). Joyce seems to have copied down notes from Renan's *Life of Jesus* in Stanislaus's diary; see *Oeuvres,* 1:1584–86.
30. His manuscript now in the Cornell Joyce Collection (Robert Scholes, *The Cornell Joyce Collection* [Ithaca: Cornell University Press, 1961], n.10) is dated January 10th 1900.
31. Seamus Clandillon, 1878–1944, was a member of the Gaelic League and a singer interested in folk music. He was to become Director of Broadcasting, Irish Free State, 1925–34.
32. Eugene Sheehy, in *Centenary History of the Literary and Historical Society of University College Dublin, 1855–1955,* ed. James Meenanil Tralee (Kerryman, n.d.), 84–85. Reprinted in *Workshop,* 152–53.
33. *SH,* 90–98.
34. Henrik Ibsen, *The Wild Duck, The Master-Builder, Ghosts,* and *Pillars of Society.*
35. Hegel, *Esthétique,* 3:258–59.
36. Friedrich Wilhelm Nietzsche, *The Birth of Tragedy* (New York: Doubleday & Co., 1956), passim.
37. Butcher, chap. 7.
38. *SH,* 30: "what he now regarded as the hell of hells—the region, otherwise expressed, wherein everything is found to be obvious."
39. Bosanquet, 151–65.
40. Ibid., 155.
41. Ibid., 162:

> We are accustomed—to regard Shakespeare mainly as the creator of our present poetic world, and the inaugurator of our national greatness in the field of literature. Now in one sense this is all very true. He forms the most brilliant starting-point of our literary art, just as Newton does of our science and Locke of our philosophy. But if we think that our art and its conditions are continuous with his art and its conditions, and that the perception of beauty as a living and active force was awakened in his time and has had a continuous development from then till now, in that case I imagine we are deceived. Within the history of the concrete feeling for beauty, to which poetry, and especially the drama, belongs on one side, though it also borders closely upon the province of intellect, Shakespeare in every way marks not the opening but the closing of a period.

42. This reservation explains Joyce's later interest in Ben Jonson, from whose writings he tried to draw theoretical as well as poetic inspiration. See Richard Ellmann, *James Joyce* (1959; rev. ed., London: Oxford University Press, 1982), 120, 127.

43. Bosanquet, 162–63.
44. *CW,* 42: "If a sanity rules the mind of the dramatic world there will be accepted what is now the faith of the few, there will be past dispute written up the respective grades of *Macbeth* and *The Master Builder.* The sententious critic of the thirtieth century may well say of them—Between him and these there is a great gulf fixed."
45. *CW,* 42.
46. Alfred de Musset, *Rolla,* 1: "Je suis venu trop tard dans un monde trop vieux."
47. The allusion is ambiguously to Hans Jaeger's *La Bohème de Christiana,* which raised a scandal in 1885, as well as to Murger's *La Vie de Bohème,* still very popular at the end of the century.
48. Hegel, *Esthétique,* 1:222.
49. For Richard Wagner's criticism of fashion in *The Art-Work of the Future,* trans. W. A. Ellis (London: Kegan Paul, Trench, Trübner & Co., 1892), vol. 1 of *Prose Works,* 1:5.
50. Bosanquet, 343–44.
51. *CW,* 42: "Drama is essentially a communal art and of widespread domain. The drama—its fittest vehicle—almost presupposes an audience, drawn from all classes. In an art-loving and art-producing society the drama would naturally take up its position at the head of all artistic institutions."
52. *CW,* 42: "Let us criticize in the manner of free people, as a free race, recking little of ferula and formula. The Folk is, I believe, able to do so much. *Securus judicat orbis terrarum* is not too high a motto for all human art-work."
53. *CW,* 43. For another topical allusion to Wagner, see *CW,* 45, the presentation of *Ghosts* as "a deepset branch of the tree, Igdrasil, whose roots are stuck in earth, but through whose high leafage the stars of heaven are glowing and astir," an echo of Wagner's *The Art-Work of the Future,* 197.
54. Ellmann, *James Joyce,* 137.
55. *MBK,* 117–18. Stanislaus continues: "He was habitually a very late riser, but wherever he was, alone in Paris, or married in Trieste, he never failed to get up at about five in all weathers to go to the early morning Mass on Holy Thursday and Good Friday. Resenting my sarcasms at Trieste, he asked me:
   - You think I am too orthodox, don't you?
   - No, but I think you've seen the performance before.
   - So you have seen 'Norma' before."

Joyce was not strikingly original in his comparison of drama and the Mass. See, for example, Stéphane Mallarmé's "Offices" (*La Revue Blanche,* 1895), in *Oeuvres,* 388–97.
56. Bosanquet, 151–52 (italics mine).
57. Ibid., 153 (italics mine):

> The *Divine Comedy* . . . is absolutely *unique in form.* By setting the traditional classifications at defiance it raised, at the outset of modern art, *the fundamental aesthetic problem whether art-species are permanent.* All this significance is lost if we go about in a half-hearted way to effect an approximation between it and an epic or a tragedy. And being unique, it is a very type of individuality. It is, says Fraticelli, "a political, historical and ethical picture of the thirteenth century." Although it is such a picture, it yet has its central interest in the fate of souls, and more particularly in that of the poet's soul. Nothing could be more universal, and nothing could be more individual, nothing even more personal. It is the climax of the long movement which we have attempted to trace, in which *the individual spirit has deepened into a universe within because it has widened into oneness with the universe without.*

58. Bosanquet, 157. See also 156–57 (italics mine):

> Dante's subject-matter is nominally the other world. . . . This primary peculiarity colors his whole artistic scheme. Unity and symmetry of parts in the whole, which to him, as to the earlier mediaeval writers, constituted beauty, is no doubt the ultimate burden of his thought, but the vehicle of its expression is a dualism. In this it represents the mediaeval or early modern mind whose utterance it was. The same fate had befallen the kingdom of heaven that befel Plato's ideas. The very principle of unity itself was hardened into something material, at all events into something sensuous, and was set in opposition over against that of which it was meant to be the unity, as "another" world against "this." . . . This first dualism between our world of images and the other world of images, forms the content of Dante; but beside and behind it there is also another, the dualism of the entire universe of sense-images over against its spiritual or moral meaning.

Quite predictably, Bosanquet also quotes Dante's letter to Can Grande on fourfold interpretation.
59. Bosanquet, 159.
60. See "The Holy Office," in *CW,* 149–52.
61. Bosanquet, 2.
62. Hegel as quoted in ibid., 476.
63. Frank Budgen, *James Joyce and the Making of "Ulysses"* (Blooming-

ton: Indiana University Press, 1960; rev. ed., London: Oxford University Press, 1972), 187: "He was not a great admirer of Wagner."

64. See the reference to *Lohengrin* in *CW,* 45.

65. Bosanquet, 342–43 (italics mine). A long note quotes Hegel's *Aesthetic,* 1:212, on Dutch painting.

66. Bosanquet deals with it on the very next page (344): "Joyce had been reading him rather closely—."

67. James Joyce, "A Portrait of the Artist" (1904), in *Workshop,* 64.

68. Ibid. See also *SH* and *PA,* passim.

69. See Bernard Baas and Armand Zaloszyc, *Descartes et les fondements de la psychanalyse* (Paris: Navarin-Osiris, 1988).

CHAPTER THREE
Ibsen: Hail and Farewell

1. See *SH,* 40–41; Richard Ellmann, *James Joyce* (1959; rev. ed., London: Oxford University Press, 1982), passim; and Constantine Curran, *James Joyce Remembered* (London: Oxford University Press, 1968), chap. 6.

2. *CW,* 47–48.

3. In the present case, but also when Joyce wrote to Ibsen in March 1901; see *Letters,* 1:51–52.

4. Later in Zurich Joyce demonstrated to a friend Ibsen's superiority over Shakespeare: see Ellmann, *James Joyce,* 398.

5. *CW,* 51: "There is something untrue lying at the root of their union."

6. A word that curiously prefigures the suspicion of "idle words" in the priest of "The Sisters," in *Dubliners,* a book in which "idle promises" is a constant theme.

7. *CW,* 61: "She had been tempted to kill him in frenzy when he spoke of their connection as an episode in his life." But this time the link is clearly established between hallucination and murderous desire.

8. See the description of Leopold Bloom as "the new womanly man" in *U,* 493.

9. T. S. Eliot, "Notes on *The Waste Land,*" in *Collected Poems, 1909–1935* (London: Faber & Faber, 1936), 80.

10. *CW,* 53: "[Meeting Irene] he begins to think seriously on himself, his art, and on her, passing in review the course of his life

since the creation of his masterpiece, 'The Resurrection Day.' He sees that he has not fulfilled the promise of that work, and comes to realize that there is something lacking in his life."

11. Jacques Lacan, "La fonction de la beauté: Barrière extrême à interdire l'accés à une horreur fondamentale, Kant avec Sade," in *Ecrits* (Paris: Le Seuil, 1966), 775. See also Jacques Lacan, *Le Séminaire, Livre VII: L'Ethique de la psychanalyse*, ed. Jacques-Alain Miller (Paris: Le Seuil, 1986), 279–80.

12. See the final page of "The Dead."

13. See also *CW*, 65: "Ibsen's drama . . . is wholly independent of his characters," and 67: "Ibsen has striven to let the drama have perfectly free action."

14. Bosanquet, 157.

15. Ibid., 152.

16. *SH*, 40–41 (italics mine).

17. The double pamphlet was distributed by the two authors in person and by Stanislaus, who could remember delivering a copy to George Moore's maidservant.

18. According to Curran (*James Joyce Remembered*, 116–17), Joyce had read some of Björnstjerne Björnson, as well as Georg Brandes's study of Ibsen and Björnson, available at the National Library. As early as 1901 Joyce owned a copy of *Over Aevne (Beyond Human Forces)*, a drama that, according to D. B. Christiani (*Scandinavian Elements of "Finnegans Wake"* [Evanston: Northwestern University Press, 1965]), may well have served as an inspiration for the Nameless One, the "man in the macintosh" of *Ulysses*.

19. Giuseppe Giacosa (1867–1906) will reappear about a decade later in the preliminary notes to *Exiles*.

20. Jose Echegaray y Eizaguirre (1832–1916), whose neoromantic subjects are sometimes adaptations from Ibsen's dramas.

21. Curran (*James Joyce Remembered*, 9) has informed us that he possessed a number of Maeterlinck's works signed and dated 1899 by Joyce: *Alladine and Palomides, Interior, The Death of Tintagile* (London, 1899), and *Pelleas and Melisande, The Sightless*, trans. Laurence Alma Tadema (London, n.d.).

22. Although Joyce's spelling points to Jakob Jakobsen, which may be analyzed as a Freudian slip evocative of self-begetting, the actual reference is to Jens Peter Jacobsen (1867–1885), whose novel *Niels Lyhne* was to be found in Joyce's library as *Siren Voices*, trans. E. F. L. Robertson (London, Heinemann, 1896). See his letter to Stanislaus Joyce, 28 February 1905, in *Letters*, 2:83.

23. Joyce's interest in Hauptmann had first made itself felt the preceding year. Curran (*James Joyce Remembered,* 9) has informed us that he kept a copy, signed and dated Feb. 1900 by Joyce, of *The Coming of Peace,* a translation by Janet Achurch and C. E. Wheeler (London, 1900), as well as another, dated August 1900, of *Hannele: A Dream Poem (Hanneles Himmelsfahrt),* a translation by William Archer (London, n.d.). For a substantial study of Hauptmann's impact on Joyce, see Marvin Magalaner, *Time of Apprenticeship* (New York: Abelard Schuman, 1959).

24. Indeed, Joyce can be quite lucid about Hauptmann. See his letter to Stanislaus Joyce, 9 October 1906, in *Letters,* 2:173.

25. The very same year, 1901, while at Mullingar with his father, Joyce had tried his hand at translating *Vor Sonnenaufgang,* Hauptmann's success of twelve years earlier, as well as his latest play, *Michael Kramer,* 1900. Still a novice in German, Joyce met with the additional difficulty of Hauptmann's Silesian dialect, which he rendered as countrified Anglo-Irish; he had, however, to leave some pages blank, temporarily as he thought. His manuscript translation of *Vor Sonnenaufgang* is in the Huntington Library and has been edited and presented by Jill Perkins (Canoga Park, Calif.: PSP Graphics, 1978).

26. Magalander, *Time of Apprenticeship,* 62–63: "What is original, genuine, deep and strong is born only in isolation. The artist is always a real hermit . . . I can forgive anything, except vulgarity."

27. Umberto Eco, "Joyce et D'Annunzio," in *Joyce* (Aix-en-Provence: Cahiers de l'Arc, 1968).

28. The editors of *CW* note that Joyce probably borrowed the quotation from I. Frith, *Life of Giordano Bruno the Nolan* (London, 1887), 165, in which Bruno is quoted: "No man truly loves goodness and truth who is not incensed with the multitude."

29. See Curran, "Joyce's D'Annunzian Mask," in *James Joyce Remembered;* and the early (1904) "Portrait of the Artist": "The air of false Christ was manifestly the mask of a physical decrepitude" testifies to Joyce's searing self-doubt as to his birthright.

30. *U,* 207: "Fatherhood is a mystical estate, an apostolic succession from only begetter to only begotten."

31. The theme is central to the *Portrait of the Artist,* in which it is the occasion of several variations, from Parnell as "uncrowned king of Ireland" to "The Holly and the Ivy."

32. Joyce had assigned one of these emblems (for, after, all there is more than one type of crown: of laurel, of thorns, etc.) to John

Ruskin, for whom he is supposed to have written the funeral trib-
ute "A Crown of Wild Olives" (an allusion also to Ruskin's book)
soon after his death on 20 January 1900.

33. Maurice Blanchot, *L'Entretien infini* (Paris: Gallimard, 1969).

34. *Letters,* 2:8–9.

35. *MBK,* 115–16.

36. Lacan, *Le Séminaire, Livre VII: L'Ethique de la psychanalyse.*

CHAPTER FOUR

"James Clarence Mangan"

1. The Dublin lecture was delivered to the Literary and Historical
Society of University College on 15 February 1902 and was published the following May in *St. Stephen*'s 1, no. 6 (1902): 116–
18. No manuscript has survived. The Trieste lecture, "Giacomo
Clarenzio Mangan," was delivered five years later, in 1907; its incomplete, heavily corrected manuscript (in the Slocum Collection, Yale University Library) appears in a facsimile edition in the
volume entitled *Notes, Criticism, Translations and Miscellaneous
Writings* in *James Joyce Archive,* general ed. Michael Groden (New
York: Garland, 1977–80), 131–36.

2. *MBK,* 112 and 183.

3. *MBK,* 133; and *Workshop,* 191–92.

4. *Workshop,* 78.

5. *Workshop,* 215.

6. *MBK,* 168.

7. An additional indication that Joyce had a personal involvement
with James Clarence Mangan is that the Irish poet, at the time,
was better known and respected than he suggests and did not really need hagiography. Lionel Johnson, an active member of the
Irish Literary Society, was one of his fervent admirers. Louise
Guiney had edited a selection of his poems in 1897, and D. J.
O'Donoghue had devoted a volume to his life and writings the
same year. Two editions, one of his prose works, the other of his
poetry, were being prepared and were published in 1903 and
1904, respectively.

8. See *SH,* 78: "Classicism is not the manner of any fixed age or of
any fixed country: it is a constant state of the artistic mind."

9. See *SH,* 79: "To many spectators the dispute had seemed a dispute about names, a battle in which the position of the standards

152

could never be foretold for a minute. Add to this internecine warfare—the classical school fighting the materialism that must attend it, the romantic school struggling to preserve coherence—and behold from what ungentle manners criticism is bound to recognize the emergence of all achievement."

10. Walter Pater, *Appreciations, with an Essay on Style,* vol. 1 of *Works,* 10 vols. (1889; Library edition, London: Macmillan, 1910), 241:

> The words, *classical* and *romantic,* although, like many other critical expressions, sometimes abused by those who have understood them too vaguely or too absolutely, yet define two real tendencies in the history of art and literature. Used in an exaggerated sense, to express a greater opposition between those tendencies than really exists, they have at times tended to divide people of taste into opposite camps. But in that *House Beautiful,* which the creative minds of all generations—the artists and those who have treated life in the spirit of art—are always building together, for the refreshment of the human spirit, these oppositions cease; and the *Interpreter* of the *House Beautiful,* the true aesthetic critic, uses these divisions, only so far as they enable him to enter into the peculiarities of the objects with which he has to do. The term *classical* fixed, as it is, to a well-defined literature and a well-defined group in art, is clear indeed; but then it has often been used in a hard and merely scholastic sense by the praisers of what is old and accustomed, at the expense of what is new, by critics who would never have discovered for themselves the charm of any work, whether new or old, who value what is old, in art or literature, for its accessories, and chiefly for the conventional authority that has gathered about it. . . . And as the term, *classical,* has been used in a too absolute, and therefore in a misleading sense, so the term *romantic,* has been used much too vaguely, in various accidental senses. . . . The romantic spirit is in reality, an ever-present, an enduring principle, in the artistic temperament; and the qualities of thought and style which (some) uses of the word *romantic* really indicate, are indeed but symptoms of a very continuous and widely working influence. . . .
>
> Though the words classical and romantic, then, have acquired an almost technical meaning, in application to certain developments of German and French taste, yet this is but one variation of an old opposition which may be traced from the very beginning of the formation of European art and literature. From the first formation of anything like standard of taste in these things, the restless curiosity of their more eager lovers necessarily made itself felt, in the craving for new motives, new subjects of interest, new modifications of style. Hence, the opposition between the classicists and the romanticists—

between the adherents, in the culture of beauty, of the principles of liberty, and authority, respectively—of strength, and order or what the Greeks called *kosmiotes.*

It is probably on the following page that Joyce found the notion of the classical temper as "the romantic temper grown old," in Stendhal's famous definition: "Romanticism is the art of presenting to people the literary works which, in the actual state of their habits and beliefs, are capable of giving them the greatest possible pleasure; *classicism,* on the contrary, of presenting them with that which gave the greatest possible pleasure to their grandfathers."

Later on, Pater, following Stendhal's lead, insisted that there were "the born romanticists and the born classicists." In particular, romanticism, "although it has its epochs, is in its essential characteristics rather a *spirit* which shows itself at all times, in various degrees, in individual workmen and their work, and the amount of which criticism has to estimate in them, taken one by one, than the peculiarity of a time or a school. Depending on the varying proportion of curiosity and the desire of beauty, natural tendencies of the artistic spirit at all times, it must always be partly a matter of individual *temperament*" (italics mine).

11. Matthew Arnold, "The Study of Poetry," in *Matthew Arnold's Essays in Criticism* (New York: Dutton, 1964), 239.

12. Bosanquet, 49: "Outside Plato's definite theory of art the beautiful is principally spoken of as the manifestation of intelligence (*Cratylus* 416)."

13. Quoted in Bosanquet, 114 (italics mine).

14. Ibid. (italics mine).

15. G. W. F. Hegel, *The Introduction to Hegel's "Philosophy of Fine Art,"* translated from the German, with notes and prefatory essay, by Bernard Bosanquet (London: Kegan Paul, Trench, Trübner & Co., 1886), 169ff. Quoted in Bosanquet, 487.

16. Bosanquet, 486 (italics mine).

17. Whatever may have been the impact of Arthur Symons's *The Symbolist Movement in Literature* (London: William Heinemann, 1899), which has been well documented.

18. Bosanquet, 143 (italics mine).

19. Plato, *Republic,* book 7.

20. *U,* 186.

21. G. W. F. Hegel, *Esthétique,* 3rd ed., 4 vols. (Paris: Aubier, 1944), 1:100: "[L'Idéal est] l'Idée réalisée conformément à son concept:

... il doit y avoir une adéquation complète entre l'Idée et sa forme, en tant que réalité concrète."

22. Bosanquet, 474.

23. Bosanquet (476) uses the word "unrest" to characterize symbolic art.

24. Bosanquet, 363: "The root of mysticism is a love of directness amounting to impatience, and a repugnance to *the circuitous approaches of systematic thought*" (italics mine).

25. Plato, *Republic,* 3:400b and d.

26. Bosanquet, 36, in which Bosanquet agrees with Plato heartily.

27. Bosanquet, 49.

28. Ibid., 164.

29. Symons, *The Symbolist Movement in Literature,* 77–102.

30. This is the basis of Lacan's distinction between sign and signifier.

31. See *CW,* 76.

32. See *CW,* 76–77.

33. Shelley was only a stage in Joyce's personal development. See *MBK,* 112: "He had progressed from his boyish hero-worship of Byron through Shelley to Blake." This is why the references to Shelley in the *Portrait of an Artist* need to be put into perspective.

34. Percy Bysshe Shelley, *English Critical Essays* (Oxford University Press, 1916), 156.

35. However, Joyce remained less than enthusiastic. See *MBK,* 140; and Richard Ellmann, *James Joyce* (1959; rev. ed., London: Oxford University Press, 1982), 99: "Joyce was skeptical of Theosophy as being a recourse for disaffected Protestants." See also *U,* 191–92.

36. Also to be observed in Stephen Dedalus's remark about Shakespeare: "Loss is his gain," *U,* 197.

37. Bosanquet, 183.

38. Michel de Certeau, *L'Ecriture de l'histoire* (Paris: Gallimard, 1975), 10.

39. *PA,* 205.

40. See *An. Post.* II.

41. *De An.* 407a.

42. Compare the temptation of Christ, a scene that fascinated Joyce (*SH,* 222) as a crucial moment in the story and process of salvation.

43. See Jacques Lacan, *Le Séminaire, Livre VII: L'Ethique de la psychanalyse,* ed. Jacques-Alain Miller (Paris: Le Seuil, 1986), chap. 11, and *Le Séminaire, Livre XX: Encore,* ed. Jacques-Alain Miller (Paris: Le Seuil, 1975), passim.

44. Lacan, *Le Séminaire, Livre VII: L'Ethique de la psychanalyse,* 248 (translation mine).
45. See F. S. L. Lyons, *Ireland since the Famine* (London: Weidenfeld & Nicholson, 1971, 1973), chap. 4, "The Battle of Two Civilizations," and *SH,* chap. 14, and in *PA,* 251–52.
46. "The Bruno Philosophy," in *CW,* 133.
47. Bosanquet, 478.
48. *Workshop,* 30–33.

CHAPTER SIX
The Pola Notebook and Aquinas

1. See under "Thomas Aquinas" in Bibliography.
2. William T. Noon, *Joyce and Aquinas: A Study of the Religious Elements in the Writing of James Joyce* (New Haven: Yale University Press; London: Oxford University Press, 1957), 20.
3. Aristotle, *Nicomachean Ethics,* Loeb Classical Library, 3.
4. Noon, *Joyce and Aquinas,* 41.
5. Annie Tardits, "L'Appensée, le renard et l'hérésie," in *Joyce avec Lacan,* ed. Jacques Aubert (Paris: Navarin Editeur, 1987), 131.
6. François Regnault, "Méditations sur le Somme," *Ornicar?* 2 (March 1975): 13–18.
7. Stanislaus Joyce, in *The Complete Dublin Diary of Stanislaus Joyce,* ed. George H. Healey (Ithaca: Cornell University Press, 1971), 4, reports his brother's pronouncement: "when the bard begins to write he intellectualizes himself."

Conclusion

1. See the 1904 "Portrait of the Artist," in *Workshop,* 67: "even his rhetoric proclaimed transition."
2. Walter Pater, *The Renaissance: Studies in Art and Poetry,* vol. 9 of *Works,* 10 vols. (London: Macmillan, 1910), 49. Quoted in Wolfgang Iser, *Walter Pater: The Aesthetic Moment,* trans. David H. Wilson (Cambridge: Cambridge University Press, 1987), 30.
3. Ibid., 54–56. Quoted in Iser, *Walter Pater: The Aesthetic Moment,* 40.
4. Matthew Arnold, especially in *Essays in Criticism: Second Series,* 1888, might be found to be the originator of notions in Joyce's

critical writings (the references are to *Selected Prose* [London: Penguin Library, 1970]): "interpreter," 158; "classicism," 344, 357, and 365ff.; "laws," 362; "men of letters," 358; and Leopardi, 398.

5. See, for example, this analysis of the Mass in the *Encyclopaedia Britannica:* "The service of the mass contains in itself dramatic elements, and combines with the reading out of portions of Scripture by the priest, its epical part, a lyrical one in the anthems and responses of the congregation."

6. Yrjö Hirn, *The Origin of Art: A Psychological and Sociological Inquiry* (London: Macmillan, 1900).

7. Jacques Lacan, "Introduction de la Chose," in *Le Séminaire, Livre VII: L'Ethique de la psychanalyse,* ed. Jacques-Alain Miller (Paris: Le Seuil, 1986), chaps. 4 and 5.

8. See Serge André, "Joyce le symptôme, Hugo le fantasme," in *Le Part de l'Oeil* (Brussels: Presses de l'Académie Royale des Beaux-Arts), no. 4 (1988): 109–13.

9. Jacques Lacan, "Séminaire Le Sinthome," 17 February 1976, in *Ornicar?* 11. Joyce's problem is that "un certain rapport à la parole lui est de plus en plus imposé au point qu'il finit par dissoudre le langage lui-même."

10. Jacques Aubert, "Réflexions sur Joyce et l'occultisme," in *Studies on Joyce's "Ulysses,"* ed. Jacqueline Genet and Elisabeth Helle-gouarc'h (Caen: Université de Caen, 1991).

11. Thomas Common, *Nietzsche as Critic, Philosopher, Poet and Prophet: Choice Selections from His Work* (London: Grant Richards, 1901), 142.

12. Several publications had revived interest in Spinoza at the turn of the century: *The Ethic of Benedict de Spinoza,* trans. W. Hale-White and Amelia H. Stirling, 2d ed. (London: Duckworth & Co., 1894); Sir Frederick Pollock, *Spinoza, His Life and Philosophy* (London: Duckworth & Co., 1899); and Harold H. Joachim, *A Study of the Ethics of Spinoza* (Oxford: Clarendon Press, 1901).

13. Common, *Nietzsche as Critic, Philosopher, Poet and Prophet,* 142, quoting Nietzsche, *The Birth of Tragedy,* 5 and 24: "The joy which the tragic myth creates has the same origin as the joyful sensation of dissonance in music."

14. Annie Tardits, "L'Appensée, le renard et l'hérésie," in *Joyce avec Lacan,* ed. Jacques Aubert (Paris: Navarin Editeur, 1987),.

15. See Joyce's letter to Carlo Linati about *Ulysses,* 21 September 1920, *Letters,* 1:146–47.

16. *James Joyce in Padua,* ed., trans., and with an Introduction by Louis Berrone (New York: Random House, 1977).

17. Augustine, *Confessions* 7.12. Quoted in the 1904 "Portrait of the Artist" (*Workshop,* 65) and in *U* (142).

18. *SH,* 211: "It was for the man of letters to record these epiphanies with extreme care."

19. *SH,* 32: "He put his lines together not word by word but letter by letter. He read Blake and Rimbaud on the value of letters and even permuted and combined the five vowels to construct cries for primitive emotions."

20. Luc Ferry, *Homo Aestheticus* (Paris: Grasset, 1990), 47–48.

21. Michel de Certeau, *L'Ecriture de l'histoire* (Paris: Gallimard, 1975).

22. There is every reason to believe that Joyce quite early consulted and used Henry Noel Humphreys, *The Origin and Progress of the Art of Writing* (London: Ingram, Cooke & Co., 1853); see *Oeuvres,* ed. Jacques Aubert (Paris: Gallimard, 1982), 1:1743–44.

23. See Jean-Guy Godin, "Du symptôme à son épure: Le sinthome," in *Joyce avec Lacan.*

APPENDIX A
Aristotle: The Paris Sources

1. Herbert Gorman, *James Joyce* (New York: Reinhart, 1940), 94, probably extrapolating from Joyce's own words, wrongly assumes that Cousin, not Barthélémy-Saint-Hilaire, was Aristotle's French translator. Cousin's speciality was Plato, and the volume under discussion is his only excursion into peripatetic philosophy. Gorman's (and possibly Joyce's) misapprehension may be due to the fact that the Bibliothèque Nationale Catalogue lists the book under "Aristotle."

2. Victor Cousin, *De la Métaphysique d'Aristotle: Rapport sur le concours ouvert par l'Académie des Sciences Morales et Politiques, suivi d'un essai de traduction du premier et du douzième livres de la "Métaphysique"* (Paris: Ladrange, 1838).

3. Cousin, *De la Métaphysique d'Aristotle,* 1–2:

   1) Faire connaître cet ouvrage [la *Métaphysique*] par une analyse étendue et en déterminer le plan; 2) en faire l'histoire, en signaler l'influence sur les systèmes ultérieurs dans l'antiquité et les temps

modernes; 3) de rechercher et discuter la part d'erreur et la part de vérité qui s'y trouvent, quelles sont les idées qui en subsistent encore aujourd'hui, et celles qui pourraient entrer utilement dans la philosophie de notre siècle.

4. Cousin, *De la Métaphysique d'Aristotle,* 96:

L'auteur's s'efforce de prouver que la matière dans la métaphysique péripatéticienne joue à peu près le même rôle que l'idée dans la doctrine de Platon. Or la matière n'est rien que par les déterminations que la forme lui impose, comme la forme n'existe pas séparée de la matière. La forme péripatéticienne, c'est précisément l'élément d'individualité dans les choses. Dans la logique, c'est l'élément de la différence; et, comme dans le monde extérieur, c'est la forme qui fait la réalité, de même dans la logique, c'est la différence et non pas le genre qui caractérise essentiellement le défini. L'essence est donc dans la différence, dans l'individualité. La matière n'est donc qu'une simple possibilité d'être; la forme est ce qui réalise cette possibilité, et lui donne l'actualité: la forme est une énergie . . . ; c'est l'élément actif.

5. However, Joyce does not seem to have found any use for Charles Magloire Bénard's *L'Esthétique d'Aristote* (Paris, 1887), which is hardly surprising because Bénard is quite critical of modern interpretations of Aristotle.

6. Aristotle, *La Poétique d'Aristote,* new edition and translation, with a philosophical study by Adolphe Hatzfeld and Médéric Dufour (Lille: Le Bigot Frères, 1899), 1: "Toutes les parties de ce vaste ensemble . . . ne peuvent être appréciées à leur juste valeur que par les rapports intimes qu'elles ont les unes avec les autres et avec la pensée générale qui les tient étroitement unies."

7. Ernest Renan, *Averroës et l'averroïsme,* 3rd ed. (Paris: Michel Lévy Frères, 1886).

8. *CW,* 160.

9. *U,* 28.

10. *U,* 25–26.

11. See Richard Ellmann, *James Joyce* (1959; rev. ed., London: Oxford University Press, 1982), 340.

12. Karl Marx, "Preface," in *Capital: A Critical Analysis of Capitalist Production,* translated from the 3rd German edition by Samuel Moore and Edward Aveling, and edited by Frederick Engels, 2 vols. (London: Swan Sonnenschein, Lowrey & Co., 1887), xxviii.

APPENDIX B

Quotations from Aristotle in Joyce's 1903–1904 Notebooks

The present text of Joyce's notes is reprinted from Richard F. Peterson, "More Aristotelian Grist for the Joycean Mill," *James Joyce Quarterly* 17, no. 2 (Winter 1980): 213–16. The sources were published for the first time in partial form in Jacques Aubert, *Introduction à l'esthétique de James Joyce* (Paris: Didier, 1973), then in full in Joyce's *Oeuvres*.

1. *U,* 26: "The soul is in a manner all that is: the soul is the form of forms."
2. See ibid.
3. See *U,* 37: "Snotgreen, bluesilver, rust: colored signs. Limits of the diaphane. But he adds: in bodies."
4. See *PA,* 208: "Aristotle's entire system of philosophy rests upon his book of psychology and that, I think, rests on his statement that the same attribute cannot at the same time and in the same connection belong to and not belong to the same subject."
5. Compare *PA,* 139: "But does that part of the body understand or what?"
6. See *U,* 25: "It must be a movement then, an actuality of the possible as possible. Aristotle's phrase formed itself within the gabbled verses and floated out into the studious silence of the library of Saint *[sic]* Genevieve where he had read . . ."

BIBLIOGRAPHY

•

Books

Andler, Charles. *Nietzsche*. 3 vols. Paris: Gallimard, 1958.

Aristotle. *Psychologie d'Aristote: Traité de l'Ame*. Translated into French for the first time, with definitive notes by J. Barthélémy-Saint-Hilaire. Paris: Librairie Philosophique Ladrange, 1846.

———. *Psychologie d'Aristote: Opuscules (Parva Naturalia)*. Translated into French for the first time, with definitive notes. Paris: Dumont, 1847.

———. *Aristotle's Psychology in Greek and English*. With Introduction and Notes by Edwin Wallace. Cambridge: Cambridge University Press, 1882.

———. *La Poétique d'Aristote*. New edition and translation, with a philosophical study by Adolphe Hatzfeld and Médéric Dufour. Lille: Le Bigot Frères, 1899.

———. *Les Problèmes d'Aristote*. Translated by J. Barthélémy-Saint-Hilaire. Paris: Hachette, 1891.

———. *Traité de l'âme*. Translated by M. Rodier. Paris: Leroux, 1900.

———. *Métaphysique*. Translated by J. Tricot. Paris: Vrin, 1953.

———. *Ethique de Nicomaque*. Translated by J. Voilquin. Paris: Garnier-Flammarion, 1965.

———. *De l'Ame*. Edited by A. Jannone, with translation and notes by E. Barbotin. Paris: Société d'Edition "Les Belles-Lettres," 1966.

Atherton, J. S. *The Books at the Wake*. London: Faber & Faber, 1959. Expanded and corrected ed., Mamaroneck, N.Y.: Paul P. Appel, 1974.

Atti del Third International James Joyce Symposium. Trieste: Università degli Studi, Facoltà di Magistero, 1974.

Aubert, Jacques, ed. *Joyce avec Lacan*. Paris: Navarin Editeur, 1987.

Baas, Bernard, and Armand Zaloszyc. *Descartes et les fondements de la psychanalyse*. Paris: Navarin-Osiris, 1988.

Bayer, Raymond. *L'Esthétique mondiale au XXiéme siècle*. Paris: Presses Universitaires de France, 1961.

Beja, Morris. *Epiphany in the Modern Novel*. London: Peter Owen, 1971.

Bénard, Charles Magloire. *L'Esthétique d'Aristote*. Paris, 1887.

Bernard, Claude. *Introduction à l'étude de la médecine expérimentale*. Paris, 1865.

Bernays. *Zwei Abhandlungen über die Aristotelische Theorie des Drama*. 1857.

Blanchot, Maurice. *L'Entretien infini*. Paris: Gallimard, 1969.

Bosanquet, Bernard. *A History of Aesthetic*. 1892. Reprint. London: Macmillan, 1904.

Bréhier, Emile. *La Philosophie de Plotin*. Paris: Boivin, 1928.

———. *Histoire de la Philosophie*. Paris: Presses Universitaires de France, 1932; rev. ed., 1968.

Brucke, E., and H. Helmholtz. *Principes des Beaux-Arts*. Paris: Librairie Germer Baillière & Co., 1881.

Bruyne, Edgar de. *L'Esthétique du Moyen-Age*. Louvain: Editions de l'Institut Supérieur de Philosophie, 1947.

Budgen, Frank. *James Joyce and the Making of "Ulysses."* Bloomington: Indiana University Press, 1960; rev. ed., London: Oxford University Press, 1972.

Butcher, S. H. *Aristotle's Theory of Poetry and Fine Art*. London: Macmillan, 1895; rev. ed., 1902.

Buttigieg, Joseph A. *"A Portrait of the Artist" in Different Perspective*. Athens: Ohio University Press, 1987.

Byrne, John Francis. *Silent Years: An Autobiography with Memoirs of James Joyce and Our Ireland*. New York: Farrar, Straus & Co., 1953.

Callahan, Edward F., Jr., "James Joyce's Early Aesthetic." Ph.D. diss., University of Wisconsin, 1957. *Dissertation Abstracts* 17, 1957.

Cazamian, Madeleine L. *Le Roman et les idées en Angleterre*. 3rd ed. Paris: Les Belles-Lettres, 1935.

Christiani, D. B. *Scandinavian Elements of "Finnegans Wake."* Evanston: Northwestern University Press, 1965.

Colum, Mary. *Life and the Dream*. Dublin: Dolmen Press, 1966.

Common, Thomas. *Nietzsche as Critic, Philosopher, Poet and Prophet: Choice Selections from His Works*. London: Grant Richards, 1901.

Cope, Jackson I. *Joyce's Cities: Archeologies of the Soul*. Baltimore: Johns Hopkins University Press, 1981.

Copleston, W. L. *A History of Philosophy.* Westminster, Md.: Newman Press, 1950.

Courtney, W. L. *The Idea of Tragedy in Ancient and Modern Drama.* Westminster: Archibald Constable & Co., 1900.

Cousin, Victor. *De la Métaphysique d'Aristote: Rapport sur le concours ouvert par l'Académie des Sciences Morales et Politiques, suivi d'un essai de traduction du premier et du douzième livres de la "Métaphysique."* Paris: Ladrange, 1838.

Cross, Richard K. *Flaubert and Joyce: The Rite of Fiction.* Princeton: Princeton University Press, 1971.

Curran, Constantine. *James Joyce Remembered.* London: Oxford University Press, 1968.

D'Annunzio, Gabriele. *Le Feu.* Translated by G. Hérelle. Paris: Calmann-Lévy, 1931.

Decaudin, Michel. *La Crise des valeurs symbolistes: Vingt ans de poésie française.* Toulouse: Privat, 1960.

de Certeau, Michel. *L'Ecriture de l'histoire.* Paris: Gallimard, 1975.

Deleuze, Gilles. *Nietzsche et la philosophie.* Paris: Presses Universitaires de France, 1962.

———. *Différence et répétition.* Paris: Presses Universitaires de France, 1968.

Eco, Umberto. *The Aesthetics of Chaosmos: The Middle Ages of James Joyce.* Translated by Ellen Esrock. Tulsa: University of Tulsa, 1982.

Eliot, T. S. *Knowledge and Experience in the Philosophy of F. H. Bradley.* London: Faber & Faber, 1964.

Ellmann, Richard. *The Identity of Yeats.* New York: Oxford University Press, 1954.

———. *James Joyce.* London: Oxford University Press, 1959; rev. ed., 1982.

———. *The Consciousness of Joyce.* London: Faber & Faber, 1977.

Encyclopaedia Britannica. 9th ed., s.v. esp. "Aesthetics," "Aquinas," "Bruno," "Cartesianism," "Drama," "Image-worship," "Poetry," and "Scholasticism."

Farmer, Albert J. *Le Mouvement esthétique et décadent en Angleterre, 1873–1900.* Paris: Librairie ancienne Honoré Champion, 1931.

Ferry, Luc. *Homo Aestheticus.* Paris: Grasset, 1990.

Foucault, Michel. *Les Mots et les choses.* Paris: Gallimard, 1966.

———. *The Order of Things.* London: Tavistock Publications, 1970.

Frith, I. *Life of Giordano Bruno the Nolan.* London, 1887.

Frontisi-Ducroux, Françoise. *Dédale: Mythologie de l'artisan en Grèce ancienne.* Paris: Maspéro, 1975.

Gilson, Etienne. *Matières et formes*. Paris: Librairie Philosophique Vrin, 1964.

Givens, Seon, ed. *James Joyce: Two Decades of Criticism*. New York: Vanguard Press, 1948.

Goldberg, L. S. *The Classical Temper: A Study of James Joyce's "Ulysses."* London: Chatto & Windus, 1961.

Goldmann, Arnold. *The Joyce Paradox: Form and Freedom in His Fiction*. London: Routledge & Kegan Paul, 1966.

Gorman, Herbert. *James Joyce*. New York: Rinehart, 1940.

Harkness, Marguerite. *The Aesthetics of Dedalus and Bloom*. Lewisburg, Pa.: Bucknell University Press, 1984.

Hayman, David. *Joyce et Mallarmé*. Paris: Les Lettres Modernes, 1956.

Hegel, G. W. F. *Cours d'esthétique*. Translated by Charles Magloire Bénard. 5 vols. Paris and Nancy, 1840–52.

———. *The Introduction to Hegel's "Philosophy of Fine Art."* Translated from the German, with notes and prefatory essay, by Bernard Bosanquet. London: Kegan Paul, Trench, Trübner & Co., 1886.

———. *Esthétique*. 4 vols., 3rd ed. Paris: Aubier, 1944.

———. *Aesthetic*, part 2. Translated by William M. Bryant. New York: Appleton & Co., 1879.

Hegel, G. W. F., and C. L. Michelet. *The Philosophy of Art: An Introduction to the Scientific Study of Aesthetics*. Translated from the German by William Hastie. Edinburgh: Oliver & Boyd, 1886.

Hirn, Yrjö. *The Origin of Art: A Psychological and Sociological Inquiry*. London: Macmillan, 1900.

Houang Kia Tcheng. *Le Néo-Hégélianisme en Angleterre*. Paris: Librarie philosophique Vrin, 1954.

Howarth, Herbert. *The Irish Writers*. New York: Hill & Wang, 1958.

Humphreys, Henry Noel. *The Origin and Progress of the Art of Writing*. London: Ingram, Cooke & Co., 1853.

Hurll, Estell M. *The Madonna in Art*. London: David Nutt, 1899.

Iser, Wolfgang, *Walter Pater: The Aesthetic Moment*. Cambridge: Cambridge University Press, 1987.

Jolas, Maria. *A James Joyce Yearbook*. Paris: Transition Press, 1949.

Joyce, James. *Ulysses*. New York: Random House, 1934; reset and corrected, 1961.

———. *Stephen Hero*. Edited by John Slocum and Herbert Cahoon. New York: New Directions, 1944; rev. ed., 1963.

———. *Letters of James Joyce*. Edited by Stuart Gilbert (vol. 1, 1957) and Richard Ellmann (vols. 2 and 3, 1966). 3 vols. New York: Viking Press.

————. *The Critical Writings of James Joyce*. Edited by Ellsworth Mason and Richard Ellmann. New York: Viking Press, 1959.

————. *A Portrait of the Artist as a Young Man: The Definitive Text, Corrected from the Dublin Holograph*. By Chester G. Anderson and edited by Richard Ellmann. New York: Viking Press, 1964.

————. *The Workshop of Daedalus: James Joyce and the Raw Materials for "A Portrait of the Artist as a Young Man."* Collected and edited by Robert Scholes and Richard M. Kain. Evanston: Northwestern University Press, 1965.

————. *Oeuvres*. Edited by Jacques Aubert. Vol. 1. Paris: Gallimard, Bibliothèque de la Pléiade, 1982.

Joyce, Stanislaus. *My Brother's Keeper: James Joyce's Early Years*. Edited, with an Introduction, by Richard Ellmann, and with a Preface by T. S. Eliot. London: Faber & Faber, 1958.

————. *The Complete Dublin Diary of Stanislaus Joyce*. Edited by G. Healey. Ithaca: Cornell University Press, 1971.

Kain, Richard. *Dublin in the Age of William Butler Yeats and James Joyce*. Norman: University of Oklahoma Press, 1962.

Lacan, Jacques. *Ecrits*. Paris: Le Seuil, 1966.

————. *Le Séminaire, Livre XX: Encore*. Edited by Jacques-Alain Miller. Paris: Le Seuil, 1975.

————. "Séminaire R. S. I." *Ornicar?* 2 (March 1975) to 5 (Winter 1976–77).

————. "Séminaire Le Sinthome." *Ornicar?* 6 (March-April 1976) to 11 (September 1977).

————. *Le Séminaire, Livre VII: L'Ethique de la psychanalyse*. Edited by Jacques-Alain Miller. Paris: Le Seuil, 1986.

Ladous, Régis. *Le Spiritisme*. Paris: Le Cerf, 1989.

Lehmann, A. G. *The Symbolist Aesthetic in France, 1885–1895*. Oxford: Basil Blackwell, 1950; 2d ed., 1968.

Leopardi, Giacomo. *Essays and Dialogues*. Translated, with a Biographical Sketch, by Charles Edwardes. London: Trübner & Co., 1882.

Levin, Harry. *James Joyce*. 2d ed. London: Faber & Faber, 1960.

Lyons, F. S. L. *Ireland since the Famine*. London: Weidenfeld & Nicholson, 1971; rev. ed., 1973.

Lyons, J. B. *James Joyce and Medicine*. Dublin: Dolmen Press, 1973.

McGrath, F. C. *The Sensible Spirit: Walter Pater and the Modernist Paradigm*. Tampa: University of South Florida Press, 1986.

Magalaner, Marvin. *Time of Apprenticeship*. New York: Abelard Schuman, 1959.

Maritain, Jacques. *Art et scolastique*. 4th ed. Paris: Librarie de l'Art Catholique, 1920.

Marx, Karl. *Capital: A Critical Analysis of Capitalist Production*. Translated from the 3rd German ed. by Samuel Moore and Edward Aveling, and edited by Frederick Engels. 2 vols. London: Swan Sonnenschein, Lowrey & Co., 1887.

Morse, J. Mitchell. *The Sympathetic Alien: James Joyce and Catholicism*. New York: New York University Press, 1959.

Namer, Emile. *Bruno*. Paris: Seghers, 1966.

Nietzsche, Friedrich. *The Case of Wagner. Nietzsche contra Wagner. The Twilight of the Idols. The Anti-Christ*. Translated by Thomas Common. London: Henry & Co., 1896.

———. *Thus Spake Zarathoustra*. Translated and introduced by Alexander Tille. London: Henry & Co., 1896.

———. *A Genealogy of Morals*. Translated by W. A. Haussman and introduced by Alexander Tille. London: T. Fisher Urwin, 1899.

———. *Works*. Edited by Alexander Tille. *Poems,* translated by John Gray, in vol. 1, *A Genealogy of Morals,* translated by William A. Haussmann. Vol. 2, *Thus Spake Zarathoustra: A Book for All and None,* translated by A. Tille. London: Unwin, 1899. Vol. 3, *The Case of Wagner, Nietzsche contra Wagner, The Twilight of the Idols, The Anti-Christ,* translated by Thomas Common. Vol. 4, *The Dawn of Day,* translated by Johann Voltz. London: Unwin, 1899–1903.

———. *Nietzsche as Critic, Philosopher, Poet and Prophet: Choice Selections from His Works*. Compiled by Thomas Common. London: Grant Richards, 1901.

Noel, Jean. *George Moore, l'homme et l'oeuvre*. Paris: Marcel Didier, 1966.

Noon, William T. *Joyce and Aquinas: A Study of the Religious Elements in the Writing of James Joyce*. New Haven: Yale University Press; London: Oxford University Press, 1957.

O'Brien, Darcy. *The Conscience of James Joyce*. Princeton: Princeton University Press, 1967.

Ortigues, Edmond. *Le Discours et le symbole*. Paris: Aubier, 1962.

Pater, Walter. *Works*. 10 vols. Vol. 1, *Appreciations, with an Essay on Style,* and vol. 9, *The Renaissance: Studies in Art and Poetry.* 1899; Library Edition. London: Macmillan, 1910.

Peake, Charles. *James Joyce: The Citizen and the Artist*. London: Edward Arnold, 1977.

Plotin. *Ennéades*. Translated by E. Bréhier. Paris: Les Belles Lettres, 1938.

Prickard, A. O. *Aristotle on the Art of Poetry*. London: Macmillan, 1891.

Pseudo-Denys. *Oeuvres complètes*. Translated, with an Introduction and notes, by M. de Gandillac. Paris: Aubier, 1943.

Pucelle, Jean. *L'Idéalisme en Angleterre de Coleridge à Bradley*. Neufchatel: Editions de la Baconnière, 1955.

Rabaté, Jean-Michel. *James Joyce, Authorized Reader*. Baltimore: Johns Hopkins University Press, 1991.

Renan, Ernest. *Averroës et l'averroïsme*. 3rd ed. Paris: Michel Lévy Frères, 1886.

———. *L'Avenir de la Science*. Paris: Calmann-Lévy, 1890; 1900.

Reynolds, Mary T. *Joyce and Dante: The Shaping Imagination*. Princeton: Princeton University Press, 1981.

Ross, W. D. *Aristote*. Paris: Payot, 1930.

Ruskin, John. *The Works of John Ruskin*. Edited by E. T. Cook and Alexander Wedderburn. 39 vols. Library Edition. London: George Allen, 1903–12.

Stirling, James Hutchinson. *The Secret of Hegel: Being the Hegelian System in Origin, Principle, Form and Matter*. 2 vols. London: Longman, Green, Longman, Roberts & Green, 1865.

Sullivan, Kevin. *Joyce among the Jesuits*. New York: Columbia University Press, 1958.

Symons, Arthur. *The Symbolist Movement in Literature*. London: William Heinemann, 1899.

Thatcher, David S. *Nietzsche in England, 1890–1914: The Growth of a Reputation*. Toronto: University of Toronto Press, 1970.

Thomas Aquinas. *La Somme théologique de Saint Thomas, Latin-français en regard, par l'abbé Drioux*. Translated into French by Abbé Drioux. Paris: Eugène Belin, 1854.

———. *Synopsis Philosophiae Scolasticae ad Mentem Divi Thomae, ad Utilitatem Discipulorum Redacta*. 2d ed. Paris: Apud A. Roger & F. Chernoviz, editores, 1892.

Tindall, W. Y. *James Joyce: His Way of Interpreting the Modern World*. London: Charles Scribner's Sons, 1950.

Trench, Richard Chenevix. *On the Study of Words*. London: John W. Parker & Son, 1851.

Tysdahl, B. J. *Joyce and Ibsen: A Study in Literary Influence*. Oslo: Norwegian Universities Press; New York: Humanities Press, 1968.

Vinci, Leonardo da. *The Literary Works of Leonardo da Vinci*. Compiled and edited from the original manuscripts by Jean-Paul Richter. 2 vols. London: Sampson Low, Marston, Searle & Rivington, 1883.

Wagner, Richard. *The Music of the Future*. London: Schott & Co., 1873.

———. *Prose Works*. Translated by W. A. Ellis. London: Kegan Paul, Trench, Trübner & Co., 1892.

Wahl, Jean. *Les Philosophies pluralistes d'Angleterre et d'Amérique*. Paris: Alcan, 1920.

Wallace, William. *Prolegomena to the Study of Hegel's Philosophy and Especially of His Logic*. 2d ed. Oxford, 1894.

Ward, Anthony. *Walter Pater: The Idea in Nature*. London: Mac-Gibbon & Kee, 1966.

Wencelius, Léon. *La Philosophie de l'art chez les néo-scolastiques de langue française*. Paris: Jouve, 1932.

Wilde, Oscar. *Intentions: The Soul of Man under Socialism*. 1891. London: Methuen & Co., 1908.

Wilson, Edmund. *Axel's Castle*. New York: Scribner's 1931.

Yates, Frances A. *The Art of Memory*. London: Routledge & Kegan Paul, 1966.

Yeats, W. B. *Essays and Introductions*. London: Macmillan, 1961.

———. *Explorations*. London: Macmillan, 1962.

———. *Mythologies*. London: Macmillan 1962.

———. *Uncollected Prose*. Vol. 1. London: Macmillan, 1970.

———. *Uncollected Prose*. Vol. 2. London: Macmillan, 1975.

Zola, Emile. *Le Roman expérimental*. Paris, 1880.

Journals and Essays

L'Arc, no. 36, "Joyce et le roman moderne," 1968.
Athenaeum, 1896–1900.
Fortnightly Review, 1896–1900.
Revue Néo-Scolastique, 1894–95.
Savoy, 1896.

André, Serge. "Joyce le symptôme, Hugo le fantasme." In *La Part de l'Oeil*, no. 4 (1988). Brussels: Presses de l'Académie Royale des Beaux-Arts de Bruxelles.

Aubert, Jacques. "'. . . comme Spinoza' ou: Vers l'égnome du Père." Unpublished paper. Séminaire de la Bibliothèque, Ecole de la Cause Freudienne, Paris, 1987–88. "Psychose, Sinthome et Ecriture."

———. "Réflexions sur Joyce et l'occultisme." In *Studies on Joyce's "Ulysses,"* edited by Jacqueline Genet and Elisabeth Hellegouarc'h. Caen: Université de Caen, 1991.

Baker, James R. "James Joyce's Esthetic Freedom and Dramatic Art." *Western Humanities Review* 5 (Winter 1950–51): 29–40.

Beebe, Maurice. "Joyce and Aquinas: The Theory of Aesthetics." *Philological Quarterly* 36 (January 1957): 20–35.

Blissett, William. "James Joyce in the Smithy of His Soul." In *James Joyce Today: Essays on the Major Works*, edited by T. F. Staley. Bloomington: Indiana University Press, 1966.

Block, Haskell. "The Critical Theory of James Joyce." *Journal of Aesthetics and Art Criticism* 8 (March 1950): 172–84.

Brandabur, Edward. "Stephen's Aesthetic in *Portrait of the Artist as a Young Man*." In *The Celtic Cross*, edited by Ray B. Brown et al. Lafayette: Purdue University Studies, 1964.

de Certeau, Michel. S.v. "Mystique." In *Encyclopedia Universalis*.

Deleuze, Gilles. "Renverser le Platonisme." *Revue de Métaphysique et de Morale* (October–December 1966).

Dougherty, Charles T. "Joyce and Ruskin." *Notes and Queries* 118 (February 1953).

Duncan, J. E. "The Modality of the Audible in Joyce's *Ulysses*." *PMLA* 72 (March 1957): 286–95.

Evans, David. "Stephen and the Theory of Literary Kinds." *James Joyce Quarterly* 11 (Winter 1974): 165–69.

Feshbach, Sidney. "A Slow and Dark Birth: A Study of the Organization of *A Portrait of the Artist as a Young Man*." *James Joyce Quarterly* 4 (Summer 1967): 289–300.

———. "A Dramatic First Step: A Source for Joyce's Interest in the Idea of Daedalus." *James Joyce Quarterly* 8, no. 3 (Spring 1971): 197–204.

Fleming, Rudd. "*Quidditas* in the Tragi-comedy of Joyce." *University of Kansas City Review* 15 (Summer 1949): 288–96.

Godin, Jean-Guy. "Du symptôme à son épure: Le sinthome." In *Joyce avec Lacan*, edited by Jacques Aubert. Paris: Navarin Editeur, 1987.

Grayson, Thomas. "James Joyce and Stephen Dedalus: The Theory of Aesthetics." *James Joyce Quarterly* 4 (Summer 1967): 310–19.

Hardie, R. P. "The *Poetics* of Aristotle." *Mind* 4 (1895): 350–64.

Hope, A. D. "The Esthetic Theory of James Joyce." *Australasian Journal of Psychology and Philosophy* 21 (December 1943): 93–114.

Houdebine, Jean-Louis. "James Joyce: Obscénité et théologie." *Tel Quel* 83 (1980): 23–24.

———. "Joyce: Littérature et religion." *Tel Quel* 89 (1981): 41–73.

Houdebine, Jean-Louis, and Philippe Sollers. "La Trinité de Joyce, I et II." *Tel Quel* 83 (1980): 36–88.

Jacquot, Jean. "L'Esthétique de Joyce." In *Mélanges Georges Jamati*. Paris: Editions du C.N.R.S., 1956.

Kiralis, Karl. "Joyce and Blake: A Basic Source for *Finnegans Wake*." *Modern Fiction Studies* 4 (Winter 1958–59): 329–34.

Kronnegger, M. E. "Joyce's Debt to Poe and the French Symbolists." *Revue de Littérature Comparée* (April-June 1965): 243–54.

Kumar, Shiv. "Bergson and Stephen Dedalus's Aesthetic Theory." *Journal of Aesthetics and Art Criticisms* 16 (September 1957).

Lacan, Jacques. "Le rêve d'Aristote." In *Aristote aujourd'hui*, edited by M. A. Sinaceur (Paris: Erès and UNESCO, 1988).

Loss, Archie K. "Another 'Gay Science.'" *James Joyce Quarterly* 25 (Summer 1988): 511–13.

Mahaffy, Vicky. "Wagner, Joyce and Revolution." *James Joyce Quarterly* 25 (Winter 1988): 237–47.

McLuhan, Marshall. "Joyce, Aquinas and the Poetic Process." *Renascence* 4 (Fall 1951): 3–11.

Mason, Ellsworth. "Joyce's Categories." *Sewanee Review* 51 (Summer 1953): 427–32.

Millot, Catherine. "Epiphanies." In *Joyce avec Lacan*, edited by Jacques Aubert. Paris: Navarin Editeur, 1987.

Morin, Edward. "Joyce as Thomist." *Renascence* 9 (Spring 1957): 127–31.

Nietzsche, Friedrich. "The Principle of Aesthetics." *To-morrow* 4 (December 1897): 73–182.

Peterson, Richard F. "More Aristotelian Grist for the Joycean Mill." *James Joyce Quarterly* 17, no. 2 (Winter 1980): 213–16.

Piel, J., ed. "Giacomo Leopardi." *Critique* (Paris) 512–13 (January–February 1990). Special issue on Leopardi.

Poirier, Richard. "Pater, Joyce, Eliot." *James Joyce Quarterly* 26 (Fall 1988): 21–35.

Regnault, François. "Meditations sur la Somme." *Ornicar?* 2 (March 1975): 13–18.

Scholes, Robert. "Stephen Dedalus: Poet or Esthete?" *PMLA* 79 (1964).

Scotto, Robert M. "'Visions' and 'Epiphanies': Fictional Technique in Pater's *Marius* and Joyce's *Portrait*." *James Joyce Quarterly* 11 (1973): 41–50.

Senn, Fritz. "Esthetic Theories." *James Joyce Quarterly* 2, no. 2 (Winter 1965): 134–36.

Shapiro, Harold I. "Ruskin and Joyce's *Portrait*." *James Joyce Quarterly* 14 (1977): 92–93.

Silverstein, Norman. "Bruno's Particles of Reminiscence." *James Joyce Quarterly* 2, no. 4 (Summer 1965): 271–80.

Sollers, Philippe. "Joyce et Cie" and "La Voix de Joyce." In *Théorie des exceptions*. Paris: Gallimard, 1986.

Staley, T. F. "Religious Elements and Thomistic Encounters: Noon on Joyce and Aquinas." In *Re-Viewing Classics of Joyce Criticism*, edited by Janet E. Dunleavy. Champaign: University of Illinois Press, 1991.

Tardits, Annie. "Joyce en Babylonie." *Cahiers de Lectures Freudiennes* 7–8. Special issue, "Le Manque à lire." Paris: La Lysimaque, 1985.

———. "L'Appensée, le renard et l'hérésie." In *Joyce avec Lacan,* edited by Jacques Aubert. Paris: Navarin Editeur, 1987.

Tindall, William York. "James Joyce and the Hermetic Tradition." *Journal of the History of Ideas* 15 (1954).

Voelker, Joseph C. "'Nature it is': The Influence of Giordano Bruno on James Joyce's Molly Bloom." *James Joyce Quarterly* 14 (Fall 1976): 39–48.

Wulf, Maurice de. "Les théories esthétiques propres à Saint Thomas." *Revue Néo-Scolastique* 1 (1894).

INDEX

.

173

Designed by Laury A. Egan

Composed by Brevis Press in Galliard

Printed on 55 lb. Sebago Antique Cream
and bound in Joanna Arrestox cloth
by The Maple Press Company